DINOSAURS
AND OTHER PREHISTORIC CREATURES
ACTIVITY
LAB
EXCITING PROJECTS FOR
BUDDING PALEONTOLOGISTS

Senior editor Michelle Crane
Senior designer Stefan Podhorodecki
US editor Kayla Dugger
US executive editor Lori Hand
Illustrator Simon Tegg

Managing editor Francesca Baines
Managing art editor Phillip Letsu
Senior production editor Andy Hilliard
Senior production controller Jude Crozier
Jacket designer Stephanie Cheng Hui Tan
Design development manager Sophia MTT
Senior jackets coordinator Priyanka Sharma-Saddi
Jacket DTP designer Rakesh Kumar
Picture researcher Ahmad Bilal Khan

Publisher Andrew Macintyre
Art director Karen Self
Associate publishing director Liz Wheeler
Publishing director Jonathan Metcalf

Consultant Chris Barker
Photographer Nigel Wright

PRODUCED FOR DK BY:
XAB Design
Designers Nigel Wright, Jan Browne
Art direction Nigel Wright
Project creation Nigel Wright
Project editor Stephanie Farrow

First American Edition, 2022
Published in the United States by DK Publishing
1745 Broadway, 20th Floor, New York, NY 10019

A catalog record for this book
is available from the Library of Congress.
ISBN: 978-0-7440-5070-7

DK books are available at special discounts when purchased
in bulk for sales promotions, premiums, fund-raising,
or educational use. For details, contact:
DK Publishing Special Markets,
1745 Broadway, 20th Floor, New York, NY 10019
SpecialSales@dk.com

Printed and bound in China

For the curious
www.dk.com

Smithsonian

The Smithsonian
Established in 1846, the Smithsonian is the world's largest
museum and research complex, dedicated to public education,
national service, and scholarship in the arts, sciences, and
history. It includes 19 museums and galleries and the
National Zoological Park. The total number of artifacts,
works of art, and specimens in the Smithsonian's
collection is estimated at 154 million.

SMITHSONIAN

DINOSAURS

AND OTHER PREHISTORIC CREATURES

ACTIVITY

LAB

EXCITING PROJECTS FOR
BUDDING PALEONTOLOGISTS

CONTENTS

STEM FACTS
This symbol highlights extra information that explains the learning behind a project.

PREHISTORIC FACTS
This symbol flags up extra information about life in the prehistoric world.

WARNING
This symbol identifies a task that might be dangerous. Be sure to get adult supervision.

A WORD ABOUT GLUES

Several of the projects in this book require the use of glue. We have suggested that you use ordinary white glue or glue sticks, but in some cases it will be easier to use a glue gun if you have one, as this glue dries much faster. A glue gun should only ever be used by an adult, and they must be sure to follow the manufacturer's guidelines.

DINOSAUR FUN

In this chapter, you'll find fun projects to fill your world with prehistoric creatures, from flapping *Pteranodons* soaring overhead to dino-egg bath bombs that "hatch" tiny dinosaurs into the water. Build a *Triceratops* head that bursts through your wall, or make a mask and tail to become a *Tyrannosaurus*. Get measuring, cutting, folding, curling, gluing, slotting, taping, sewing, painting, squishing, stuffing, and building as you make these exciting dinosaur projects!

GLOWING WORLDS
PREHISTORIC LANTERN

Prehistoric creatures didn't all live at the same time, or in the same type of terrain. Which of your favorites lived alongside each other? Did they live in the forest, ocean, or desert? You can make these glowing lanterns to recreate their worlds.

Pliosaurs and other marine reptiles could "swim" around a deep blue ocean lantern.

Think about scale (how big the shapes need to be in relation to each other).

Use a background color to show water, forest, or desert, for example.

Make string handles for your lantern, or use it as a nightlight by your bed.

Cut out silhouettes of creatures, plants, and mountains.

MAKE YOUR OWN
PREHISTORIC LANTERN

This project shows you how to make a forest lantern using a large jar and green tissue paper. To make a different one, just change the color of the paper (blue for ocean, for example, or orange for a hot desert world) and research different template shapes.

Kentrosaurus

Time 90 minutes, plus drying time

Difficulty Easy

Tendaguripterus

Veterupristisaurus

WHAT YOU NEED

Green tissue paper

Large glass jar approx. 7 in (18 cm) high and 3½ in (9 cm) across

White glue

2 pieces of black paper (one big enough to go around the jar)

Dicraeosaurus

Paintbrush

Pencil

String

Ruler

Scissors

Battery-powered tea light

Giraffatitan

TEMPLATES

For our lantern, we used the creatures above, which all shared the same habitat at the same time, but if you want, you can research your own favorites. Remember to keep the templates in proportion so the silhouettes are the correct size compared to each other.

Rough, uneven squares will create interesting light effects.

1 Tear up a large sheet of tissue paper into small squares, about 1 in x 1 in (2 cm x 2 cm). Don't worry about making the squares neat.

2 Paint glue on a section of the inside of the jar and then use your brush to stick squares over the glue. Work on a small area at a time.

Keep working in small sections until the whole jar is covered.

3 Smooth the paper down with more glue and overlap the edges so that there are no gaps between the squares.

4 When you get to the top of the jar, make sure you have a neat edge around the rim.

The overlapped squares of tissue paper create different strengths of color.

5 Let the inside of the jar dry while you measure out your silhouettes.

6 Measure the height of the jar and divide that measurement in half to determine how wide to make your strip of black paper.

Trim the strip of paper to length.

7 Cut a strip of black paper as wide as the measurement in step 6 and long enough to fit around the jar with an overlap of about ⅖ in (1 cm).

8 On the strip, sketch out the landscape you want for your prehistoric creatures. You could draw a few bushes or even a hill.

Some dinosaur plant foods, such as ferns, still grow on Earth today.

9 Cut out your strip of landscape and paint glue onto the back of it.

10 Stick the strip around the jar (near the base, but where the side is still flat).

If you find drawing difficult, trace the shapes instead or use the grid method on page 17.

The huge neck of *Giraffatitan* accounted for half its total length.

12 Cut out the *Giraffatitan* silhouette. Paint glue onto the back of it and carefully add it to the scene.

11 Copy the template of the *Giraffatitan* onto black paper. (Remember to think about the scale of the dinosaur and the height of the jar.)

13 Repeat steps 11–12 to copy the other silhouettes on page 10 and glue them around the side of the jar.

Tie each end of the handle loosely so you can adjust later if necessary.

5½ in (14 cm)

14 Cut a length of string 24 in (65 cm) long to go around the jar, and another 12 in (30 cm) long for the handle. Tie the ends of the handle to the long piece, about 5½ in (14 cm) apart.

15 Wrap the long piece of string twice around the neck of the jar and knot tightly. Adjust the handle knot positions if necessary and then tighten. Switch on the tea light and place it inside.

16 Hang the lantern up or put it by your bed for some dino-dreams.

With its head 39 ft (12 m) above ground, *Giraffatitan* towered over most of its neighbors.

PREHISTORIC WORLD
WHERE DID DINOSAURS LIVE?

Dinosaurs made their home in lots of different habitats across the planet, from arid desert plains and lush forests to even polar regions. Some lived along rivers or lakes, or roamed floodplains and swamps, while for others coastal shores and lagoons provided the right kind of habitat.

STEGOSAURUS WORLD

This armored dinosaur lived 150–145 million years ago during the Jurassic Period. Using a clever grid technique to copy the shapes and make them bigger or smaller, you can build your own 3D *Stegosaurus* and even create a mini Jurassic world out of cardstock.

Many Jurassic trees were similar to the trees we have now.

Learn how to use scale to make your stegosaurs different sizes.

Cut out mountain shapes
in different colors to
make a backdrop.

Stegosaurus is famous
for the double row of
bony plates on its back.

Stegosaurus used
its spiked tail to
defend itself.

MAKE YOUR OWN
3D MODEL STEGOSAURUS

🕐	Difficulty gauge
Time	**Difficulty**
90 minutes	Medium

The secret to scaling a shape is to draw a grid so you can make something bigger or smaller while keeping everything in proportion. The scale factor is the amount you increase or decrease the size by. Here, it is 1:4—each ²⁄₅ in (1 cm) square on the template is equal to 1½ in (4 cm) on your grid. Afterward, you can change the scale to create a herd of different-sized stegosaurs.

The squares on the template are ²⁄₅ in x ²⁄₅ in (1 cm x 1 cm).

WHAT YOU NEED

Ruler

Scissors

Eraser

Pencil

Triangle

Marker

Double-sided adhesive tape

Colored cardstock

TEMPLATE 1

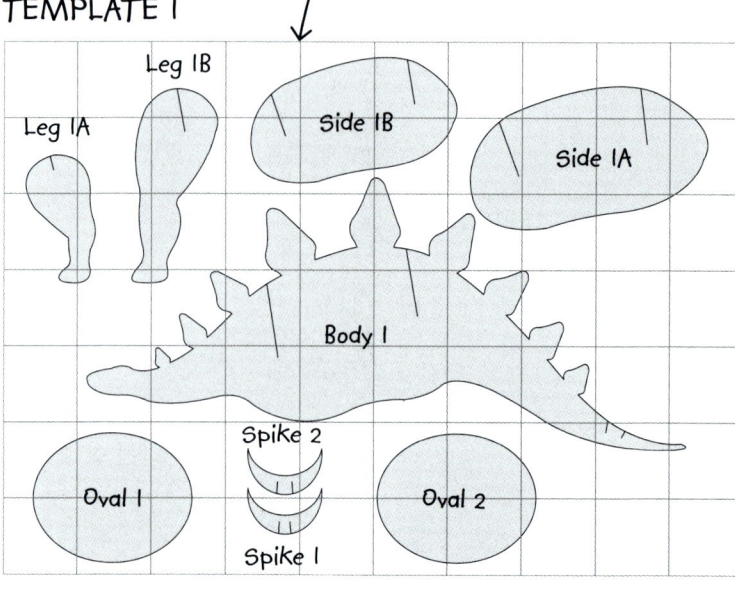

Leg 1B

Leg 1A

Side 1B

Side 1A

Body 1

Spike 2

Oval 1

Oval 2

Spike 1

TEMPLATE 2

These straight lines show where you will need to cut slots into the shape.

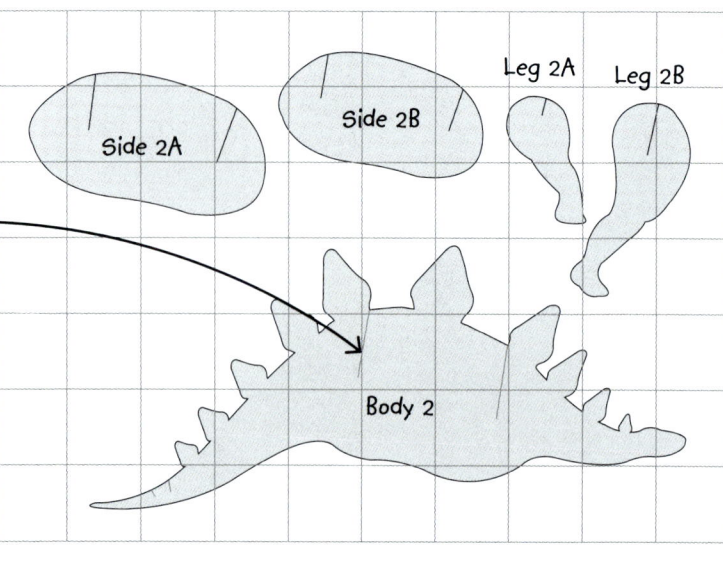

Side 2A

Side 2B

Leg 2A

Leg 2B

Body 2

Using a triangle will help you keep your corners at 90° right angles.

1 On a large sheet of cardstock, draw in pencil a rectangle 15 in (40 cm) wide and 10½ in (28 cm) high.

10½ in (28 cm)

15 in (40 cm)

2 Along the long and short edges of your rectangle, make marks every 1½ in (4 cm).

Working in small sections will help you copy each shape precisely.

1½ in (4 cm)

1½ in (4 cm)

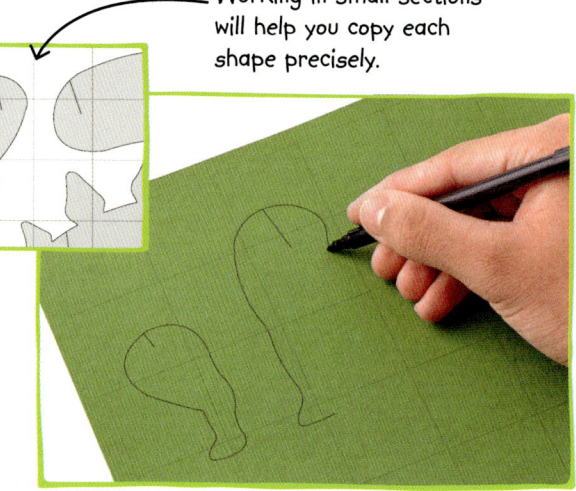

The scale factor here is 1:4. Each square on the template is four times bigger on your grid.

3 Draw horizontal and vertical lines in pencil to join up the marks and create a grid of 10 squares across and 7 down. Use the triangle to check that the lines are all at right angles.

4 With a pen (or pencil if you prefer), copy the shapes on Template 1 onto the cardstock. Working one square at a time, use the gridlines to help you copy the shapes and slots of the template.

The gridlines will help you copy the shape accurately.

5 When you have copied all the shapes on Template 1, lightly label them in pencil so you know what they are once they're cut out. Then, on a second piece of cardstock, repeat steps 1-5 to draw the shapes and slots on Template 2.

Remember to include the slot lines and position them carefully.

To find the middle, draw a line across the widest part and then the longest; where they cross is your center point.

6 Erase the pencil gridlines. Carefully cut out each shape along the pen lines, then cut the slots where marked. You could cut each piece out roughly first so it is easier to work with.

7 Draw a line lengthwise down the middle of Oval 1. Make a first mark ¼ in (6 mm) from one end of the line, then mark every ⅖ in (10 mm). You should have ¼ in (6 mm) left.

Use a triangle to keep all eight lines parallel to each other.

8 Position a triangle on the line and, at each mark, draw a line at right angles across to the edge. You should have eight lines in total.

9 Cut along each of those lines to the center line, making sure you don't cut too far. Then repeat steps 7–9 for Oval 2.

The sections should slide into place along the slots you cut.

10 Slide Oval 1 into the "slot" of Body 1 closest to the tail, using the fourth slot of the oval.

11 Ease the fourth slot of Oval 2 into the slot of Body 1 closest to the head. Push gently to make sure they are both firmly in place.

The bony plates on *Stegosaurus* may have helped it look bigger than it was to deter predators.

12 Position Side IA so that the two slots in it line up with the third slots in the ovals. Ease Side IA into both ovals at the same time.

13 Repeat step I2, but this time with Side IB, sliding it carefully into the second slots of the two ovals.

Hold the model carefully as you build the second side.

14 Slide Leg IA into the final slot of Oval 2 and Leg IB into the final slot of Oval I. That's the first half of your dinosaur done!

15 Turn the model over and slide Body 2 into the fifth slot of the two ovals, making sure the head faces the same way as it does on Body I.

Your 2D pieces of cardstock lock together to make a 3D dinosaur.

16 Repeat steps I2–I3 with the other two side pieces, building up the body of your *Stegosaurus*.

Stegosaurus had a very flexible tail that could swing in large arcs.

17 As for step 14, slide Leg 2B into Oval 1 and Leg 2A into Oval 2.

18 Ease the legs up or down slightly within the slots to balance your *Stegosaurus* so it can stand upright.

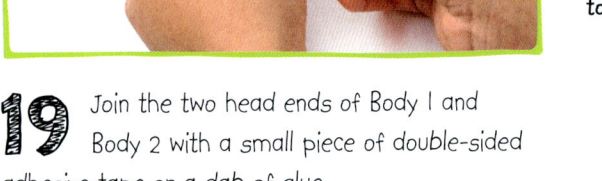

Stick the head ends of the two body pieces together.

19 Join the two head ends of Body 1 and Body 2 with a small piece of double-sided adhesive tape or a dab of glue.

20 Slide the Spike 1 piece into the two slots closest to the tail end of the main body pieces. Slide Spike 2 into the two remaining slots.

21 Finally, gently bend the "plates" slightly away from the center on both sides.

Stegosaurus plates were probably covered in keratin—the material birds' beaks are made of—and may have been brightly colored.

FEED YOUR HERD

Stegosaurs were herbivores (plant eaters), so you could make a whole forest of Jurassic trees for your herd to eat. Start with a grid of 2 in (5 cm) squares, then change the scale to make trees of different sizes.

1 Draw a grid of 2 in (5 cm) squares and copy the template above onto your grid twice.

2 Mark the red and black slots as shown, then cut out both pieces. Rub out the grid marks.

3 Cut the red slot on one piece and the black slot on the other, then slide them together.

PREHISTORIC WORLD
DINOSAUR DEFENSES

Just like animals today, dinosaurs needed defense strategies. For a few, size alone was enough to put off predators; others were small enough to hide or lived in groups for protection. Some relied on speed and others on built-in weaponry such as horns, claws, and clubbed or spiked tails. These weapons weren't just for fighting off meat eaters, though; they were often adaptations to secure mates and resources, too.

A blow from the club on the tail of an *Ankylosaurus* could shatter an attacker's bones.

Struthiomimus relied not on armor but on speed to outrun many of its predators.

Kentrosaurus was heavily armored and could use its spiked tail as a weapon.

Styracosaurus had an impressive set of horns and a defensive neck frill.

DINOSAUR HAND PUPPETS

Dinosaurs' teeth evolved to suit their diet. Those of a herbivore such as *Psittacosaurus* could cut up vegetation, while those of a carnivore such as a *Velociraptor* were more like blades for slicing meat. Why not make one of each?

The *Psittacosaurus* beak was covered in keratin, the same material that makes up feathers and claws.

Colored cardstock creates stand-out eyes and other details.

Hinged sections allow you to open and close the puppet mouths with your hand.

Both puppets have the same base model, which you can then adapt as you wish.

Use colored stickers to create the skin markings on your puppets.

Make a paper "fringe" for your *Velociraptor* feathers.

Spot the carnivore! Those sharp teeth are a giveaway ...

If you don't have colored stickers, you can just color in white stickers or paint dots onto your puppets instead.

MAKE YOUR OWN
HAND PUPPETS

Both puppets are made with the same basic template pieces below but are then adapted in different ways to make the two dinosaurs. Use the grid method on page 17 to copy the template shapes, with a scale of 1:2.

WHAT YOU NEED

Pencil

Scissors

Paintbrush

Colored cardstock

Time
2 hours

Difficulty
Medium

Ruler

Assorted colored circle-shaped stickers

White glue

BASIC TEMPLATES

Each ¾ in (2 cm) square on this template is equal to 1½ in (4 cm) on your grid.

Tab

Head
Cut x 1

The long tabs will sit outside the head and jaw pieces.

The small tabs will sit inside the head and jaw pieces.

Mouth
Cut x 1

The center fold of the mouth bends in the opposite direction to the tabs.

The tabs hold the sides in place to make the 3D head shape.

Tongue
Cut x 1

Jaw
Cut x 1

Fold lines

The side pieces fold into a three-sided box with the main jaw section.

MAKE A VELOCIRAPTOR

We used green card for the head and jaw.

1 Copy the head and jaw template shapes onto the cardstock you've chosen, scaling them up to double their size. Then cut them out.

2 Carefully crease along each of the fold lines on the head piece, bending all the tabs and sides in the same direction.

Tuck the tabs inside the head so they will be hidden when it's finished.

3 Apply glue to the tabs on the head piece, then stick them to the inside of the two rectangular sections at either end of the head piece.

4 Repeat steps 2–3 for the jaw piece, gluing the tabs to the rectangular section at one end of it to make a three-sided box shape.

We used dark red card for the mouth.

5 Copy the mouth template onto your cardstock and cut it out. Bend it along the center fold in one direction, then fold all the tabs the opposite way.

Brush glue on the outside of the two tabs near the center fold.

6 Working on one half of the mouth piece, apply glue to the inside of the three larger tabs and to the outside of the two smaller tabs.

The center fold in the mouth piece becomes a hinge.

Hold the pieces together until the glue has set firmly.

7 Position the glued tabs over the jaw piece, with the three larger tabs on the outside and the two smaller tabs tucked inside. Stick them together.

8 Repeat steps 6–7 to attach the other half of the mouth piece to the head piece, following the same positioning for the tabs.

Curl the fringes gently with your fingers to "feather" them.

9 For the fringe, cut two strips of paper 2 in x 6¾ in (5 cm x 17 cm); we made one dark green and one light green. Snip parallel cuts along each strip, about three-quarters of the way across them.

10 Glue the nonfringed edges of each strip around the head piece. Overlap them, but stick the upper strip about ⅖ in (1 cm) farther away from the edge than the lower strip.

Velociraptor teeth were serrated to tear flesh.

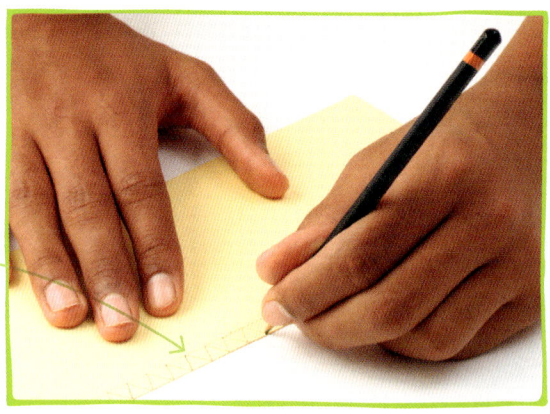

11 To make the tongue, copy the template shape onto pink cardstock. Cut it out, then glue it to the lower side of the mouth piece.

12 Draw a line 9 in (23 cm) long, ⅖ in (1 cm) from the edge of a piece of cream cardstock. Between the edge and line, draw a row of zig-zag teeth.

13 Carefully cut out the row of teeth, then repeat steps 12–13 to make a second row of teeth for the upper side of the mouth.

Starting on one side, stick the teeth over the dark-red mouth tabs.

14 Glue one row of teeth carefully over the mouth tabs around the jaw piece. Then stick the other row of teeth around the upper jaw.

Make "pupils" by sticking black dots on the cream ovals.

15 For the eyes, stick two black dots on some cream cardstock. Draw an oval around each one and cut them out.

16 Draw and cut out two slightly larger ovals on dark-red cardstock. Stick the cream ovals onto the red ones, and glue them onto the head.

17 For the nostrils, cut two small ovals from black cardstock and glue them to the top of the head. Then begin dotting on green stickers.

Add darker-colored dots toward the back of the head.

Keep the pattern random and overlap the dots sometimes.

18 Build up layers of dots to create the skin pattern. Then slide your hand inside the puppet to let your *Velociraptor* go and hunt for prey ...

ADDITIONAL TEMPLATES

These extra shapes are needed for the *Psittacosaurus*.

As before, each ¾ in (2 cm) square on this template is equal to 1½ in (4 cm) on your grid.

Tongue
Cut x 1

Cut the slots marked on each side.

Upper beak
Cut x 1

The gray areas show where you need to apply glue.

Side flap

Horns
Cut x 2

Curved beak shape

Lower beak—Cut x 1

MAKE A PSITTACOSAURUS

Stick all the mouth tabs on the inside of the head and jaw pieces for this puppet.

1 Follow steps 1–8 on pages 25–26 to make the base head, but use brown cardstock instead of green and red, and glue all the tabs inside the head.

2 Copy the upper and lower beak templates onto brown cardstock. Cut them out, including the straight slots in the upper beak piece.

Stick the side flap over the top to hide all the triangles.

Start with the slot closest to the side flap.

3 On one side of the upper *beak* piece, apply glue to the areas marked on the template. Tuck the glued triangles behind the straight cuts, one at a time, and hold in place.

4 Once all the triangles are secure, line up the side flap with the *back edge* of the upper *beak* piece and glue it in place. Hold until the glue has set.

The name *Psittacosaurus* means "parrot lizard," after its pointy beak.

5 Next, repeat steps 3–4 on the other side of the upper *beak* piece to give you a domed beak shape with both side flaps on the outside.

6 Apply glue to both sides of the upper section of the base head you made in step 1.

Press the side flaps to glue them to the sides of the base head.

7 Stick the upper beak piece to the glued sides of the upper section, pressing gently until the glue has set.

8 Apply glue to the jaw section of the base head. Stick the lower *beak* piece to it, with the curved beak shape facing upward. Hold until set.

You could draw around a coin to make your circles.

9 For the eyes, draw two circles about 1 in (2.5 cm) in diameter on pink cardstock. Then cut out the two circles.

10 Next, cut out two smaller ovals of yellow cardstock. Glue the ovals onto the pink circles, add two black dots for "pupils," and glue onto either side of the head.

11 For the nostrils, cut two small oval shapes out of black cardstock and glue them on either side of the beak, as shown.

Push the straight edge of the tongue against the fold of the mouth piece.

12 Draw and cut out a tongue from pink cardstock using the template on page 28. Glue it in position on the lower mouth piece.

Glue the tabs inside the head piece, just above the mouth hinge, one on either side.

Remember to keep the beak area free of stickers.

13 Draw and cut out the horns template shape twice on dark-brown cardstock. Fold along the tab lines and glue the tabs in place.

14 Start creating your *Psittacosaurus* skin pattern by first dotting brown stickers randomly over the head.

15 Add some pink stickers around the back of the eyes, as shown, to echo the cardstock color you used in step 9.

Too small to be used for defense, the side horns were probably for attracting a mate.

16 Add deeper-colored stickers to create darker areas around the beak and side horns. Then put your hand inside and find some leaves for your *Psittacosaurus* to chomp.

Don't forget to put stickers on the lower jaw, as well as the top of the head.

PREHISTORIC WORLD
EAT LIKE A HERBIVORE

The narrow, parrotlike beak that gave *Psittacosaurus* its name would have been used to slice off vegetation, which it would then have shredded with its small, sharp teeth. The beak may also have been used to gather seeds and was tough enough to be put to use as a nutcracker. It might even have been used to give enemies a nasty bite!

EAT LIKE A CARNIVORE

In its long, narrow snout, *Velociraptor* had jaws filled with teeth that were perfectly evolved for ripping meat off bones and carving through flesh. It had up to 56 extremely sharp teeth, each of which was a back-curved blade with serrated edges. Like most dinosaurs, the teeth were constantly replaced, so they never got blunt.

Velociraptor's large eyes may have helped it spot small prey.

Psittacosaurus skin fossils show evidence of camouflage-style pigmentation.

Its thought *Velociraptor* probably had extensive plumage.

TRICERATOPS WALL ART

Could a *Triceratops* stick its head through your bedroom wall? Very possibly! The skull of a *Triceratops* was one of the biggest and strongest of all dinosaur skulls. Its distinctive head frill and horns were all made of solid bone, but you can make this cardboard version to hang on your wall.

With some measuring and cutting out, you can turn 2D cardstock into a fearsome 3D head covered in horns and spikes.

A fringe of spikes along its frill made this young *Triceratops* look even more impressive.

Paint scaly skin on your *Triceratops* frill.

Triceratops had a parrotlike beak and lots of teeth for snipping off and grinding low-growing vegetation.

MAKE YOUR OWN
WALL-MOUNTED TRICERATOPS HEAD

This head is made from four pieces of stiff cardstock, cut to form the jaw, beak, frill, and face. The three horns are made with thinner cardstock. Carefully measure out the lines and angles to draw 2D shapes that slot together to make a 3D head.

Time 2 hours, plus painting time	**Difficulty** Hard

WHAT YOU NEED

White thin cardstock

Protractor

Pencil

Scissors

Stiff cardstock

Ruler

String

Paintbrushes

Triangle

Acrylic paints in a selection of colors

Modeling clay

Masking tape

1 First, make the jaw. Measure and cut a strip of stiff cardstock 4 in x 16½ in (10 cm x 42 cm), then fold it in half so it's 8¼ in (21 cm) long.

2 At the nonfolded end, mark a 25° angle and draw a line through it from the corner to the opposite edge. Cut both layers of card on that line.

1¾ in (4.5 cm)

3 At the folded end, mark 1¾ in (4.5 cm) from the shortest side. Draw a curved line from the mark to the far corner of the nonfolded end.

This four-sided shape, with two parallel sides of unequal length, is called a trapezoid.

4 Cut along the curved line you drew in step 3, then unfold the card. Bend it into a soft, rounded curve to form the shape of the jaw.

5 Draw a rectangle 6¼ in x 4¼ in (16 cm x 11 cm) onto stiff cardstock. At each corner of one of the long edges, draw a line up at an angle of 75° to make a trapezoid. Cut out the trapezoid.

Make two holes as shown, 1¼ in (3 cm) from the edges, to thread string through in step 35.

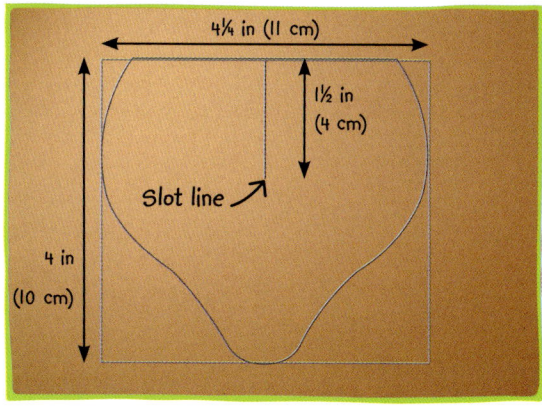

Slot line

6 Make two holes in the card with a pencil. Line up the trapezoid's short side with the jaw's straight side. Tape the angled sides of both pieces together.

7 To make the beak, measure a rectangle 4¼ in x 4 in (11 cm x 10 cm). Inside it, sketch the shape shown above. At the midpoint on the flat edge, mark a slot 1½ in (4 cm) long.

Overlapping the 2D shape along the 60° line turns it into a 3D cone.

8 Draw a diagonal line at an angle of 60° from the central end of the slot line. Cut out the full shape, then cut along the vertical slot line.

9 Align the slot edge with the 60° line and glue it in place. Tape the overlap on the underside to secure it.

Make sure the beak is attached securely.

10 On the top edge of the jaw (the curved edge), place some over-length pieces of tape, ready to attach the beak.

11 Stick the beak cone to the tape on the jaw, with the overlapping section of beak toward the back. Add more tape if necessary.

1⅓ in (3.5 cm)

These slots will support the frill of your *Triceratops*.

12 Measure 1⅓ in (3.5 cm) from the back joint of the jaw and cut a ¾ in (2 cm) slot from the top edge.

13 Repeat step 12 on the opposite side so you have two ¾-in (2-cm) long slots, one on either side of the top of the jaw.

Center line →

12 in (30 cm)

16½ in (42 cm)

Use a triangle to make sure your corners are at right angles.

The center line is at right angles to your baseline and bisects it.

1¼ in (3 cm)

2½ in (6 cm)

2½ in (6 cm)

14 To make the frill, draw a rectangle 12 in x 16½ in (30 cm x 42 cm) on stiff cardstock. Draw a vertical center line down the middle, as shown. Cut out the rectangle.

15 Draw a baseline 2½ in (6 cm) on either side of the center line, 1¼ in (3 cm) down from the top edge. From either end of that baseline, draw a line at 25° across to the top edge.

9 in (23 cm)

9 in (23 cm)

9 in (23 cm)

9 in (23 cm)

9 in (23 cm)

8 in (20 cm)

8 in (20 cm)

6¼ in (16 cm)

6¼ in (16 cm)

Center line

70°   70°

50°   50°

30°   30°

10°   10°

25°   25°

16 Turn the card around so the baseline is at the bottom. Then copy the shape above, drawing radial lines at the angles and lengths shown. Draw a spike at the end of each line. Cut around the outline of the whole shape.

Lines that all start from a central point are called radial lines.

17 Hold a ruler against each radial line in turn and lift the card up gently to neatly crease the card. Bend the whole frill slightly to give it a backward curve.

The frill will be held in place by the slots, but tape it securely, too.

18 Push the frill into the slots you cut on the top of the jaw in steps 12–13 and use tape to secure it to the jaw strip from behind.

The holes at the top are for the two long brow horns.

1¾ in (4.5 cm)

1¼ in (3.2 cm)

Center line

Mark slots on either side to attach the face to the frill.

Mark the dotted lines as guides to where you will make bends in the card.

This hole is for the short horn on the nose.

1¾ in (4.5 cm)

1¼ in (3.2 cm)

Copy this shape using the rectangle and center line as a guide.

19 To make the face, cut a rectangle 8¾ in x 11 in (22 cm x 28 cm). Draw a center line vertically down it at 5½ in (14 cm), then sketch the shapes shown above in it. (Use the grid method on page 17 if you want help with this.)

Put modeling clay behind the card for safety.

20 Carefully cut out the face shape, including the slots on either side.

21 Cut the ovals for the horns. Push a pencil through the cardstock first to make a hole through the center of the ovals, and then cut carefully around the lines.

22 Hold a ruler against one of the dotted fold lines and lift the card up gently to make a crease. Repeat for the other three fold lines.

Injuries on skull fossils of *Triceratops* suggest they may have locked horns and gouged each others' faces.

These are the measurements for the small horn.

23 To make the small front horn, draw a baseline 3 in (8 cm) long on a piece of thin white cardstock.

95°
120°
3 in (8 cm)

Line up your protractor with the left end of the baseline.

24 Mark off angles of 120° and 95° from the left end of the baseline. Draw two lines up from the left end—one line through each mark.

25 Mark a series of points 3 in (8 cm) from the left end and join them up into a curve. Cut along the baseline, curve, and 120° line.

Triceratops' horns had a solid bone core with a tough outer casing.

26 Roll the card into a cone, overlapping the baseline edge to meet the 95° line you drew. Secure it with masking tape.

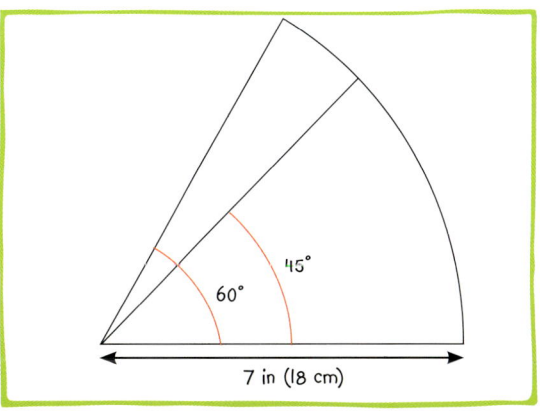

45°
60°
7 in (18 cm)

27 To make the two larger horns, follow steps 23–26, but this time using a baseline of 7 in (18 cm) and angles of 60° and 45°. Draw two.

The two sharp-tipped brow horns were up to 4 ft (1.3 m) long.

28 Cut both horns out and curve them into cones so that the baseline edges overlap with the 45° lines. Secure them with masking tape.

29 Push the small horn through the lower hole on the face and secure with masking tape on the back.

The frill slides into the slots on each side of the face piece.

30 Position the two brow horns so that they point slightly outward. Secure in place as for step 29.

31 Position the face piece over the jaw and beak. Slide the slots on either side of the face up into the frill and tape it in place on the back.

Triceratops' neck frill was made of solid bone covered in scaly skin.

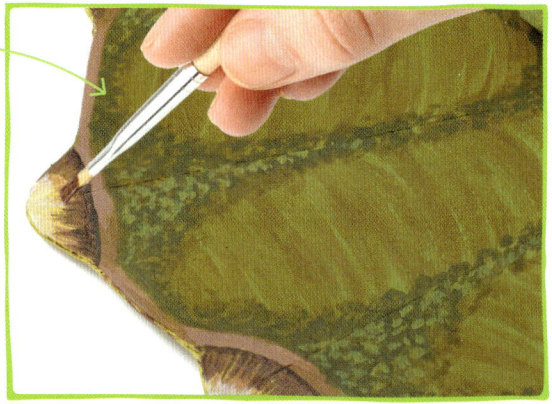

32 Paint the head with a green base coat and the horns, spikes, and beak with a cream one. Once dry, paint a pinkish edge around the frill, face, and base of the horns.

33 Dapple dark-green scaly skin markings along the radial lines, with pale-brown strokes in between. Paint brown strokes halfway up the spikes, too, as shown.

Paint the horns the same color as the frill spikes.

Only young *Triceratops* had bony spikes on their frill; as they grew older, the spikes smoothed over.

34 Paint dark- and medium-brown strokes onto the upper beak cone, as shown, and paint a matching semicircular lower beak directly onto the jaw strip.

35 Paint the horns, eyes, and nostrils and brush pale brown strokes around the face. Once dry, thread a loop of string through the two holes you made in step 6 and hang the head up on your bedroom wall.

PREHISTORIC WORLD HIDDEN CLUES

How do we know that *Triceratops* had scaly skin, horns, and a frill? Fossils can't tell us what a dinosaur's skin, coloring, or feathers were like, can it? Well, actually, yes—to some degree. Fossils of *Triceratops* skin prints show that it had scales, some of which were large and pointed. Because the horns and frill were made of very strong, solid bone, they have often survived when other parts of the dead animal simply rotted away.

Fossils of skin prints show that *Triceratops* had scaly skin.

SEW CLEVER
PLESIOSAUR KEYRING

Dinosaurs may have ruled the land on prehistoric Earth, but marine reptiles ruled the seas. Plesiosaurs were the marine giants of the waters, but this plesiosaur toy keyring is small enough to hang from a pocket or bag.

Choose a contrasting thread for the blanket stitch along the back.

Some plesiosaurs had more than 70 bones making up their long, snakelike necks.

A plesiosaur's long flippers could probably generate high speeds in short bursts.

MAKE YOUR OWN
FELT KEYRING

Felt is perfect for this project because the fibers don't fray, so your plesiosaur won't come apart. Don't worry if you're new to sewing; you'll find a guide to the stitches used on page 47.

Time 60 minutes, plus drying time

Difficulty Medium

WHAT YOU NEED

Colored felt

Tracing paper

Scissors

Pencil

Needle

Pins

Thread

8 in (20 cm) length of cord

Keyring

Craft filling

Black thread

Paintbrush

White glue

TEMPLATES

Front flipper
Cut x 2

Cut both sets of fins in dark blue felt.

Cut two in medium-blue felt.

Back flipper
Cut x 2

Body
Cut x 2

Belly
Cut x 1

Cut the belly out of a light-colored piece of felt.

Pin the tracing paper in position to help you cut accurately.

1 Trace the templates onto tracing paper and cut them out. Pin the body shape onto blue felt, then cut around it. Repeat to make a second body piece.

2 Pin the *belly* shape onto gray felt and the *flippers* onto dark-blue felt. Cut around them, then cut out eight orange ovals for body markings.

Pale bellies may have camouflaged plesiosaurs in the water.

3 Line up the flat edge of a front flipper along the *belly* edge of a *body* piece, toward the head end, and a *back* flipper nearer the tail end.

4 Position the *belly* piece over the top of the flippers. Pin through the *belly*, *flippers*, and *body* piece to hold them all in place.

This stitching will be on the inside when the keyring is finished.

This side will be on the outside when the keyring is finished.

5 Use running stitch to sew the *belly* to the *body* piece, including the flippers, as the seam will attach the pieces together. Make a finishing knot.

6 Turn the felt around the right way so you can see the outside. Check the flippers are firmly secured; add a few more stitches on the inside if not.

Make sure the two body pieces are aligned, with both heads facing the same way.

7 Turn the felt inside out. Position the two other flippers on the inside unsewn belly edge, and line up the second body piece along it, on top of them.

8 Starting at the tail end, use running stitch to sew along the belly, attaching it and the two flippers to the second body piece.

Try to make your stitches small and extra-neat near the tip of the tail.

9 Continue stitching to join the two body pieces along the neck. Make a finishing knot once you reach the end of the neck, before the head.

10 Using running stitch again, sew the other end of the two body pieces together, from the belly piece to the tip of the tail.

11 Once more, open out your plesiosaur to make sure the flippers are securely in place.

Plesiosaurs probably flapped their flippers up and down to "fly" through the water.

If a flipper doesn't feel secure, sew a few extra stitches along its seam.

This seam is on the outside of the felt, while the belly seams are hidden inside.

12 Blanket-stitch the two body pieces together along the plesiosaur's back, beginning at the tip of the tail.

13 Continue sewing until you reach a point about midway along the back, then pause—this is where you are going to insert the keyring.

Pull the ends through the loop to attach the cord.

14 Fold your cord in half. Push the looped end through the keyring, thread the ends back through the loop, and pull them to secure the keyring on the cord.

15 Tuck both ends of the cord between the two body pieces, leaving the keyring about 2 in (5 cm) above the back seam. Blanket-stitch it in place and make a finishing knot.

Sew only partway along the spine to leave an opening for stuffing.

16 Blanket-stitch from the neck around the head and along the back until you are about 1½ in (4 cm) from the keyring cord.

17 Using small amounts at a time, stuff craft filling into the opening. Use a paintbrush handle to push filling right into the head and tail.

Be careful not to pull the thread too tight or you'll distort the head.

18 When the plesiosaur is fully stuffed, continue blanket-stitching along the back to close the opening, then make a finishing knot.

19 Use black thread to sew the eyes, pushing the needle back and forth through the head to sew lots of stitches on top of each other.

20 Glue the oval back markings in place on either side of the body, then decide where you're going to hang your keyring!

Once the glue is dry, your plesiosaur is ready to hang out with ...

STITCHES YOU'LL USE

Starting Knot
Knot your thread at one end so it stays in place. If you can, "hide" the knot on the underside or inside of your fabric.

Running stitch
Push the needle in and out of the fabric, then pull the thread through. Repeat, keeping the stitches in a straight line.

Blanket stitch
Pull the thread up through the fabric, loop it around, and push the needle back through next to the stitch. Take the needle through the loop you've just made, then pull the thread tight. Continue stitching, putting your needle through the loop each time before pulling tight.

Finishing Knot
Make a stitch but, before pulling it tight, take the needle back through the loop of the stitch. Pull it tight, then repeat once more.

DINO-FEET PEN HOLDERS

Dinosaurs have left many traces on our planet, including their actual footprints fossilized in rocks. Those footprints tell us a lot about the dinosaurs who lived on Earth millions of years ago. But you can have dinosaurs roaming your desk right now with these *Allosaurus* pen holders made of papier mâché.

Allosaurus had three strong front toes, plus a small inner toe held off the ground.

Use your "feet" to keep all your pencils, pens, and brushes neat.

Papier mâché takes a while to dry, so allow time for this project.

Make the "skin" of your dino feet as smooth or as rough as you like.

MAKE YOUR OWN
DINO-FEET PEN HOLDERS

Use your measuring skills to create cardboard bases for these pen holders, then use papier mâché to build and sculpt the bases into dino feet. These steps are for *Allosaurus* feet, but you can model a different dinosaur if you wish.

Time 90 minutes, plus overnight soaking and 7 days drying time

Difficulty Medium

Warning Ask an adult for help with the hot water.

WHAT YOU NEED

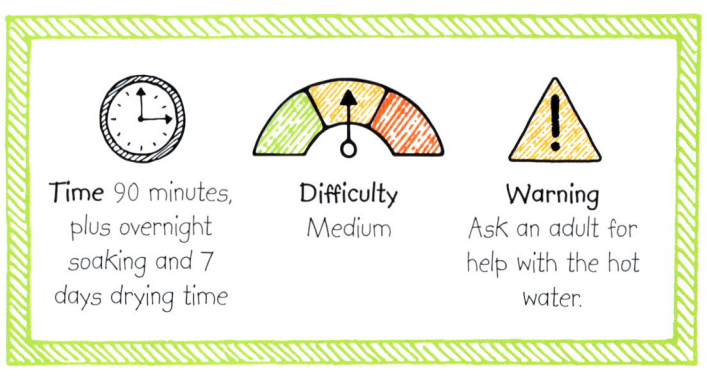

White cardstock

Wooden spoon

Large cardboard tube

Masking tape

Ruler

Newspaper

Corrugated cardboard

Paintbrushes

Mixing bowls

White glue

Acrylic paints

Pencil

Marker

Scissors

6 x small cardboard tubes

1   Make a series of marks, 4 in (10 cm) from one end, all the way around the large cardboard tube.

2   Join the marks into a line, then cut along it. If you can't get your scissors into the cardboard, poke a pencil through to make a hole. Repeat steps 1–2 at the other end of the tube for the second foot.

4 in (10 cm)

3   On the corrugated cardboard, draw around a tube. Draw a foot shape, allowing space around the tube and about 4 in (10 cm) to the middle toe.

Allosaurus was a fast hunter that ran on two hind feet.

Flipping over the first foot will make your second foot a mirror image of the first.

4 Cut out the foot and flip it over to use as a template for the other foot so you have a pair. Carefully cut out the *second* foot, too.

5 Flip the first foot back over again. Glue the end of a tube and stick it in the position you marked in step 3. Secure it in place with masking tape.

Join up the marks to draw a line parallel to the edge of the cardboard.

6 Measure along the middle toe to a point 2½ in (6 cm) from the base. (This will allow 1½ in [4 cm] for the shaping of the toe when the papier mâché goes on.)

7 Cut one of the small tubes lengthwise and lay it flat. Make a series of marks across it 2½ in (6 cm) from one end, and use a ruler to join them up into a line.

You can roll the cardboard around a pencil.

8 Using the line as a guide, cut the cardboard to size and discard the smaller piece into your recycling bin.

9 To make the base for the biggest toe, roll the cardboard into a tight tube.

10 Secure the tightly rolled cardboard with masking tape at both ends to make a cylinder about ½ in (1.5 cm) in diameter.

11 Put a line of glue along the tube and stick it in place to form the big middle toe on the top of the foot. Tape it in place.

Newspaper is fibrous and will break down easily when soaked in water.

12 Repeat steps 6–11 for the remaining toes, measuring from the tube to 1½ in (4 cm) from the tip of each toe. Then repeat steps 5–12 to make the second foot.

13 Tear the newspaper into strips about 5 in (14 cm) long, then tear the strips into small squares roughly 1 in x 1 in (2 cm x 2 cm). (Torn pieces break down better than straight-cut pieces.)

Soaking softens the paper fibers.

Dig in! Squish the mixture with your hands.

14 Put them in a large bowl and cover with boiling water. (Ask an adult to help you.) Carefully stir with a wooden spoon to make sure everything is completely wet. Leave overnight to soak.

15 The next morning, squish the pulpy mixture, rubbing it through your fingers to break down the paper fibers. Keep kneading until your papier mâché mixture has a smooth texture.

16 One handful at a time, squeeze the mixture hard to push out as much water as you can. Throw away the water you squeeze out.

Add a dollop of glue about the size of a ping pong ball.

17 Put the lumps of squeezed mixture back in the large bowl. Break them up with your hands, then add some white glue.

Use your hands to work the glue into the fibrous pulp.

18 Adding more small dollops of glue as necessary, work the mixture thoroughly until it comes together and sticks easily.

19 When ready, the papier mâché will feel like modeling clay. Then wash your hands.

All the tape will be covered up once you have applied the papier mâché.

20 Paint the cardboard base of your dinosaur foot with glue to ensure the papier mâché will stick to it.

Make the dino skin as smooth or as textured as you like.

21 Using small lumps each time, start to apply papier mâché to the base. Work along the toes first.

22 Continue applying small lumps of papier mâché to shape the foot and work up to the top of the tube.

Try to make the rim of the holder as neat and smooth as you can.

23 Finish covering the first foot, then repeat steps 20–23 for the second foot. Let them dry out. (This may take a week.) Wash your hands.

24 When the feet are completely dry, paint them inside and out with the base color you've chosen and leave to dry.

Keep the brush pretty dry to make the colors look streaky.

25 Use a smaller brush and a different color to paint the skin pattern you want on your dinosaur feet, then leave to dry.

26 To make the dinosaur's claws, paint a piece of white cardstock with streaks of two different brown paints. Leave to dry.

28 Glue each claw in place. Leave to dry, then fill the pots with your pens, pencils, and paintbrushes.

27 On the back of the cardstock, draw the shape of your dinosaur claws. Cut them out and bend each one around a pencil to give it a curve.

Push firmly to make sure the claws stick well.

STEP UP!

If you want to make a different set of feet, just vary the shape you draw in step 3 and change the shape, number, or size of the claws or hooves you make in step 27. Take a look at some of the tracks below for inspiration...

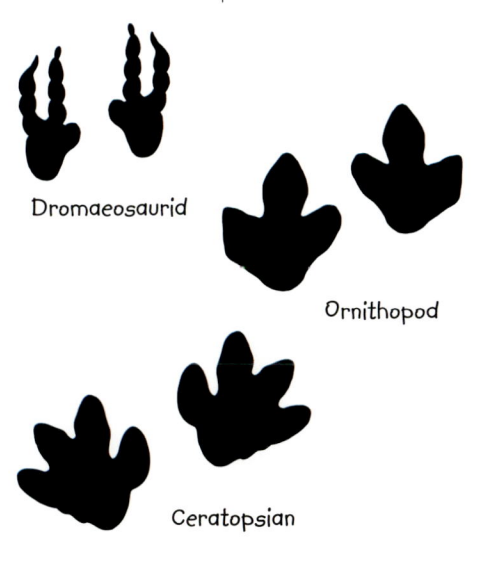

Dromaeosaurid

Ornithopod

Ceratopsian

PREHISTORIC WORLD
MAKING TRACKS

Which dinosaur made which footprint? Sauropods had flat pads, for example, while theropods such as the *Allosaurus* shown here ran on three of their toes and had vicious claws. Fossilized footprints can tell us a lot about which dinosaurs lived in herds and how fast or slow they might have been. There are even fossil footprints showing signs of broken toes and limping!

Hinged wings flap if you pull gently on the body of your *Pteranodon*.

Notches hold the string in place so your *Pteranodon* balances.

The large head crest of *Pteranodon* may have been used for display.

Pull the body down to make *Pteranodon* flap its wings.

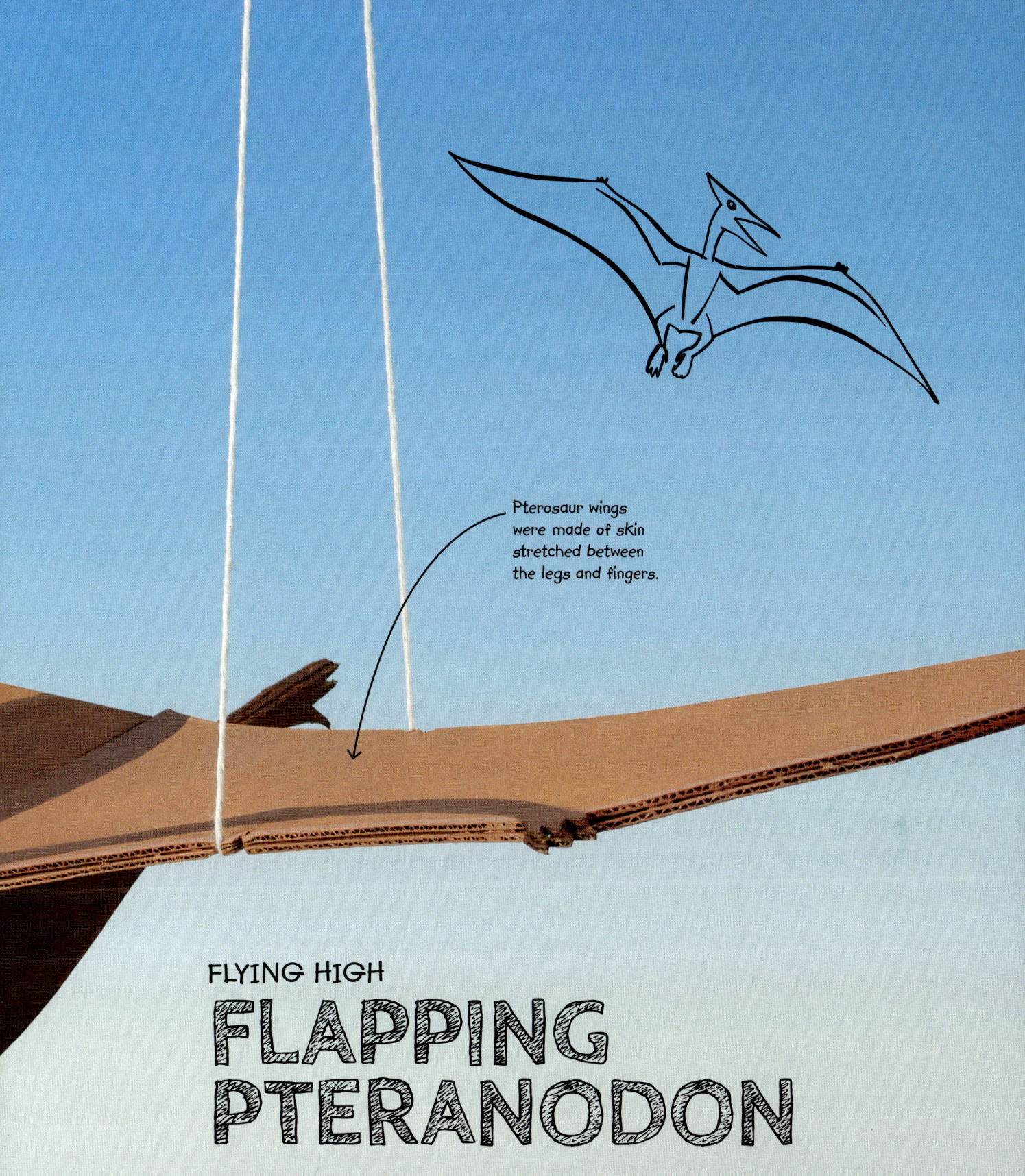

Pterosaur wings were made of skin stretched between the legs and fingers.

FLYING HIGH
FLAPPING PTERANODON

One of the largest pterosaurs, *Pteranodon* probably soared most of the time and flapped its huge wings only occasionally, but gravity and the clever hinges on this mobile mean you can flap your *Pteranodon's* wings whenever you want!

MAKE YOUR OWN
PTERANODON MOBILE

This clever mobile works with gravity. It hangs naturally at its center of gravity—the point at which it's balanced and the weight is evenly distributed. If you briefly pull it away from that point, however, the hinged wings will flap until gravity helps it regain its balance.

Time
90 minutes, plus drying time

Difficulty
Medium

Warning
Ask an adult to cut the dowel for you and hang the mobile up

WHAT YOU NEED

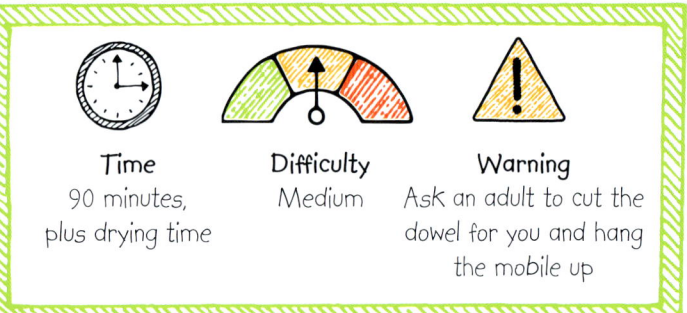

Pencil

Scissors

Paintbrushes

Craft cardstock

Acrylic paints in a variety of colors

White glue

2 x 3 ft (1 m) lengths of string

Duct tape

2 x water bottles

Ruler

Dowel

TEMPLATES

This straight "back" butts up to the wings.

Body x 3

15 in (38 cm) approximate

Wing x 4

16 in (41 cm) approximate

Use the side of the card for the straight edge of the wing.

1 Against the straight edge of the craft cardstock, draw a wing, roughly following the shape above. Use the approximate measurements above, or make your *Pteranodon* any size you want. Cut it out.

2 Using the cut-out wing as a template, draw around it three more times. Cut them all out so you have four wing pieces in total.

Using the wing to draw this line will ensure your wings butt up neatly.

3 Use a straight wing edge to draw the "back" of your *Pteranodon*. Sketch the rest of the body shape around it, roughly following the template.

4 Cut out the body shape and then use it as a template to draw around twice more. Cut both out so you have three body pieces in total.

Run the tape along the edges of the cardstock, as well as over the flat sides.

The longer curved wing side should be closest to the tail end of the body.

5 Stick duct tape along the straight edge of one wing piece, line it up with the straight back of one body piece, and tape them together.

6 Lift the wing up and lay it flat above the body. Secure it with another strip of duct tape, then fold it down *below* the body again.

The tape creates hinges that allow the wings to flap.

7 Repeat step 5 to stick a wing piece on the other side of the body. Wrap the tape over both the body and the other wing.

8 Repeat step 6 for the second wing so you have a wing on each side of the body, and tape on the top and underside of each wing.

The additional body and wing pieces cover and hide the tape.

9 Lift the wings out of the way and brush glue all over one side of the body. Stick a second body piece down onto it. Turn over and repeat on the other side with the remaining body piece.

10 Fold both wings down. Brush a wing with glue and stick one of the remaining wing pieces onto it. Repeat on the other side so each wing has two layers.

The center of gravity is where the *Pteranodon* is balanced.

11 To find the balancing points, lay your *Pteranodon* across the top of two water bottles, moving them in or out until the *Pteranodon* balances and the wings are horizontal.

12 Mark the position of the bottles and draw a line across the wing through each mark. Loop the string under each wing along the lines, then lift to check that the *Pteranodon* hangs level.

Pteranodon will hang level because its weight is evenly distributed across the strings.

13 If it doesn't hang level, repeat steps 11–12 to adjust the line positions, then cut a notch at both ends of each line to hold the string in place.

14 Paint the wings all over with medium brown and the body and tail (but not the head) with darker brown. Leave to dry.

Paint both top and underside of the wings, as you'll see both sides when the wings flap.

15 Paint the head and neck as shown, and a dark-brown outline of the body and "arms" on the wings. Once dry, add details to the head.

16 On the dowel, mark the wingspan from notch to notch. Add 2 in (5 cm) at either end and ask an adult to cut it to length for you.

Pteranodon had a wingspan of 23–30 ft (7–9 m).

Slide the knots if you need to make any last-minute adjustments for balance.

17 Tie the two loops of string to the dowel, 2 in (5 cm) from each end. Fit the wings through the loops and the string in the notches.

Your *Pteranodon* is balanced at its center of gravity—until you pull it, that is!

PREHISTORIC WORLD
WINGED REPTILES

Pterosaurs first took to the skies in the late Triassic Period and were the size of crows, with short necks, toothed jaws, and very long tails. By the late Cretaceous, they had developed toothless, beaklike jaws, the long necks and short tails that made them better fliers; and occasionally colossal proportions—*Quetzalcoatlus*, for example, had the wingspan of a small airplane (33 ft/10 m).

Pteranodon could snatch fish while it soared over the waves.

18 Hold the dowel up and let the *Pteranodon* soar. Gently pull the body from underneath to make its wings flap until it regains its balance. Then ask an adult to hang your new mobile up in your bedroom for you.

POP-UP DINOSAUR CARD

What better dinosaur to deliver a pop-up dino roar than *Parasaurolophus*? The distinctive tubelike bony crest on its head is thought to have worked like a trumpet that amplified its loud, booming calls. When you open the card, the hinged sections of the interlocking shapes let the *Parasaurolophus* pop up.

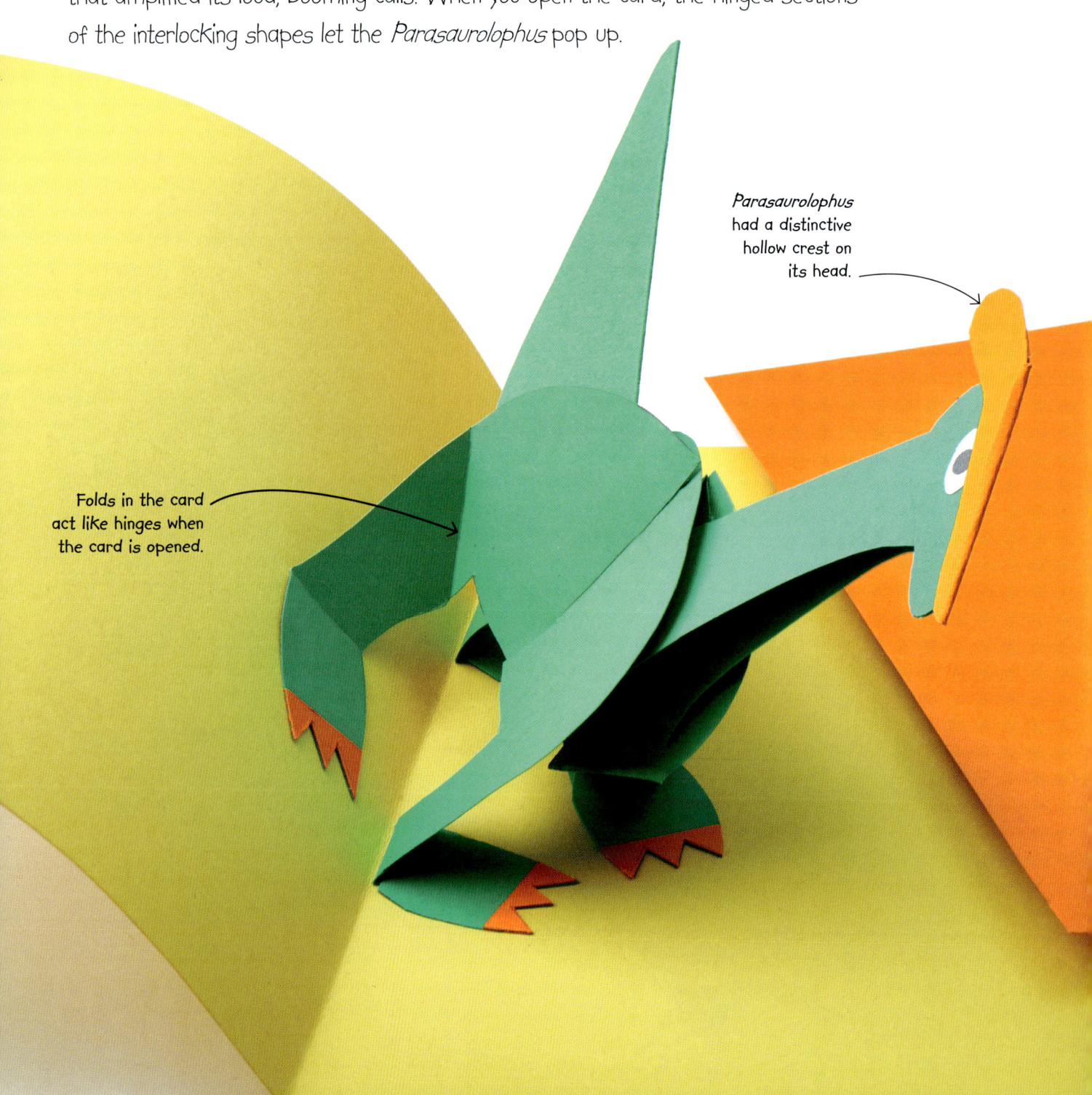

Parasaurolophus had a distinctive hollow crest on its head.

Folds in the card act like hinges when the card is opened.

Flat 2D card becomes a 3D shape when the card is opened.

The dinosaur is attached to the card by its feet.

MAKE YOUR OWN
POP-UP DINOSAUR CARD

These shapes slot together cleverly to make a *Parasaurolophus* that pops up when you open the card. The folds in the legs act as hinges that turn the interlocking 2D body shapes into a 3D dinosaur.

Time
45 minutes

Difficulty
Medium

WHAT YOU NEED

White paper

Colored cardstock

Pencil

Eraser

Triangle

Ruler

Marker

White glue

Scissors

TEMPLATES

Tab

Tail
Cut x 1

Head
Cut x 1

Tab

Body
Cut x 1 to the
black outline and
x 1 to the red
outline

Fold lines

Tab

Neck
Cut x 1

Crest
Cut x 1

Left foot
Cut x 2

Right foot
Cut x 2

1 First, make your card. Fold a 8¼ in x 11¾ in (21 cm x 30 cm) sheet of colored cardstock in half, then unfold it and mark the fold line in pencil.

2 Measure the halfway point along the fold line and use a triangle to draw an intersecting line at 90° to it.

One copy has only the black outline: Body A.

One copy has the red marks, too: Body B.

3 Copy the body template opposite, drawing two copies of it on another piece of colored cardstock. On one copy, follow the black marks only; on the other, transfer the red marks as shown.

4 Copy all the other templates, too, except the feet. Use different-colored cardstock for the crest piece. (We've used yellow, but use whatever color you like.) Carefully cut out all the pieces.

5 On the Body A piece, fold along the tabs indicated by the dotted lines. Put a dab of glue on the underside of each tab.

Position the slot in Body A along the intersecting line.

6 Line up the tab folds of Body A with the fold line on the card, and the slot in Body A with the intersecting line you drew at 90°.

These folds will act as hinges when the card is opened.

7 Bring the orange card up to the tabs and stick them to it. Fold the card over completely and press to stick the tabs down firmly.

8 Crease both legs of Body B along the red diagonal fold lines marked on the template. Fold the feet tabs in the same direction.

Note that both Body A and B are smaller on one side of the slot than the other.

9 Open the orange card. Slide Body B carefully under Body A, then unfold its legs and ease the slot on Body B up into the slot on Body A.

10 Line up the two feet tabs of Body B with the intersecting line. Fold the orange card gently to check the legs are bending correctly.

11 Unfold the card, add a drop of glue to the two tabs on Body B, then refold the card and press firmly to stick the Body B tabs to it.

12 Next, fold the neck piece firmly in half along the dotted line across the middle of the template.

Stick the neck tabs to the bigger sides of the two body pieces.

13 Open out again and fold back the end with the dotted lines marked for the tabs. Refold in half and press firmly.

14 Apply glue to the tabs of the neck. Position it, folded side upward, between Body A and Body B. Press firmly to glue in place.

Press the tail tabs to stick them to the two body pieces.

15 Fold the tail piece in half at the dotted line along the center of the template. Then open out and fold one end back along the dotted tab line. Refold in half and press firmly.

16 Glue the folded tabs on the tail and attach between Body A and Body B on the opposite side to the neck, folded side upward.

17 Carefully fold the orange card and press firmly to make sure everything is stuck together. Then reopen the card and erase the pencil lines.

Strong hind legs meant *Parasaurolophus* could probably rear up to feed on taller trees.

Wait until the glue has dried completely before erasing the pencil lines.

The head is wide at the neck end and narrow at the mouth end.

Make sure your ovals fit the head and are not too big.

18 Fold the head piece in half and press the crease down firmly. Then turn it over so the fold is upward.

19 To make eyes, draw two ovals on white paper. Draw black circles with a marker for pupils. Cut out the ovals and glue one on each side of the wide part of the head.

A tough, sharp beak helped *Parasaurolophus* crop leaves to eat.

Put the widest part of the crest at the back of the head.

20 Apply glue to the inside of the head and attach it to the top of the neck. Squeeze firmly until the glue holds the head in place.

21 Fold the yellow crest along the dotted line. Glue it on top of the head, as shown, and press firmly to stick the pieces together.

Draw the "claw" ends of the feet on the crest-colored cardstock.

22 For the feet, cut a strip of cardstock 6 in x 2 in (15 cm x 5 cm) in the main color and one half as wide in the crest color. Glue together.

23 Copy each foot template twice onto the strip, positioning the "claws" on the crest-colored strip. Cut out the four feet.

A long, heavy tail helped *Parasaurolophus* balance on its hind legs.

24 Put glue on the back of each foot and stick the four feet over the tabs at the end of the legs.

25 Carefully test that everything is folding correctly and fits within the folded card. If the tail or crest stick out slightly, you can trim them to fit. Then your dino-roar card is ready to send to a friend!

This distinctive crest could be about 3 ft (1 m) long.

PREHISTORIC WORLD
CRESTS AND CALLS

Parasaurolophus had the longest crest of any known dinosaur, but many fellow hadrosaurs also had hollow crests. These may have been used like a trumpet to make their calls louder, with the length of the crest affecting the pitch. The *Parasaurolophus* crest started growing much earlier in life compared to its close cousins, helping the crest reach such unusual proportions.

Inside the crest was an airway connecting the animal's throat to its nostrils.

EGG-STRAORDINARY
DINO-EGG BATH BOMBS

When these eggs hit the water, a chemical reaction takes place that releases fizzy bubbles of carbon dioxide gas. As the bath bombs break up, the other ingredients of your egg are released —including a hidden baby dinosaur!

The fizzing is carbon dioxide being released —that's what causes the bubbles in the bath water.

The bath bomb dissolves to "hatch" a baby dinosaur.

These eggs are delicate, so handle them just like a real egg.

MAKE YOUR OWN
DINO-EGG BATH BOMBS

These eggs fizz due to an acid-base reaction: the citric acid reacts with a base of baking soda to produce fizzy bubbles. Add an essential oil that you like the smell of, such as lemon or lavender, and food coloring to give your bath bombs some color.

1 Mix the citric acid, cornstarch, and baking soda together in a large bowl.

Time 30 minutes, plus 3 days drying time

Difficulty Easy

WHAT YOU NEED

Large bowl

Tablespoon

Teaspoon

Egg molds

Spray bottle of water

Small dinosaur toys

Essential oil

Food coloring

Whisk

⅓ cup (50 g) citric acid

3 tbsp (25 g) cornstarch

½ cup (100 g) baking soda

2 tablespoons of olive oil

Small bowl

Choose food coloring to suit the color you want for your bath bomb.

2 Measure 2 tablespoons of olive oil into a small bowl. Add a few drops of food coloring. (It won't mix well with the oil but will combine well once the dry ingredients are added later.)

Be careful—you only need a few drops of essential oil.

3 Add a few drops of an essential oil to make your bath eggs smell nice. Mix all the liquid ingredients together with your spoon.

As the liquid is added, the color of the mixture gets darker and darker.

4 Add a few drops of the oil mixture into the large bowl with the dry ingredients in it and mix them together with a whisk.

5 Continue adding small amounts of the oil mixture, a little bit at a time, and whisking in between additions.

The chemicals in this mixture will react with the bath water to release fizzy carbon dioxide bubbles.

6 Once you have finished adding the oil mixture, the ingredients in the bowl should be colored and crumbly.

7 Gently spray the mix with a fine mist spray—carefully add just a little water at a time or it will make the mixture start to fizz.

The mixture should feel damp and a bit sticky, like wet sand.

Push the mixture firmly into the mold.

8 Work the mixture together with your hands—it should just be able to stick together but still be quite crumbly.

9 Pack one half of your egg mold with the mixture. (The oil in the mixture should prevent it from sticking to the mold.)

Press hard to push the dinosaur toy up into the packed mixture.

10 Push your little dinosaur toy halfway down into the mixture inside the mold. Then pack the other half of the egg mold with mixture.

11 Line up the two halves of the mold, ready to push them together with the dinosaur hidden inside.

12 Push firmly to squeeze the two halves together, clean off the outside of the mold, then leave to set overnight.

13 Carefully remove the top half of the mold and ease the egg bomb out of the other half. Leave it to set for 1–2 days in a dry place, then pop it into your next bath and "hatch" your own baby dino.

Be very gentle, as the bath bomb might still be a bit crumbly.

PREHISTORIC WORLD
SHAPES AND SIZES

Dinosaur eggs came in various shapes and sizes. Those of an oviraptorid were long and oval, while sauropod eggs were almost spherical. Some would fit in the palm of your hand, but others were the size of a basketball—or even larger Big dinosaurs didn't necessarily lay big eggs, however; the baby dinosaurs just grew very fast once hatched.

Oviraptorid eggs were laid in a spiral pattern in the nest.

GIANT DINOSAUR EGG

All dinosaurs laid eggs, just like their closest living relatives, birds and crocodiles. And just like hens' eggs, although up to seven times bigger, some dinosaur eggs had hard, chalky shells. Make this giant dinosaur egg out of papier mâché, then try a "hatched" one—which means there'll be a baby dinosaur loose somewhere…!

You could sit your egg on a nest of twigs or leaves.

MAKE YOUR OWN
GIANT DINOSAUR EGG

To make this giant dinosaur egg, you'll need to use an inflated balloon as a model and then cover it in papier mâché. You'll need a little bit of patience, too, as you need to leave the egg to dry overnight, three times in total.

Time 3 hours, plus 3 nights drying time

Difficulty Easy

WHAT YOU NEED

Balloon

Printed and plain newsprint paper

Paintbrush

Tablespoon

String   White glue

Darning needle (or toothpick)

Sponge

Scissors

Acrylic paints

Small bowls   Pencil

1 Tear the printed newspaper into about 1½ in (4 cm) squares. You want torn, rough edges, as they will blend together well for the papier mâché.

2 Blow up your balloon. In a small bowl, mix equal amounts of glue and water. (You'll need to refill your glue solution every so often; just remember to mix equal amounts of glue and water.)

3 Paint a bit of balloon with glue, stick on a layer of overlapping paper squares, and smooth it all down with more glue. Then move on to another area.

4 Glue the squares up as close as you can to the neck of the balloon. Continue until the balloon is completely covered in newspaper and glue.

5 Repeat step 1, but this time tearing up the plain newspaper into squares. Remember, you want rough edges rather than straight ones.

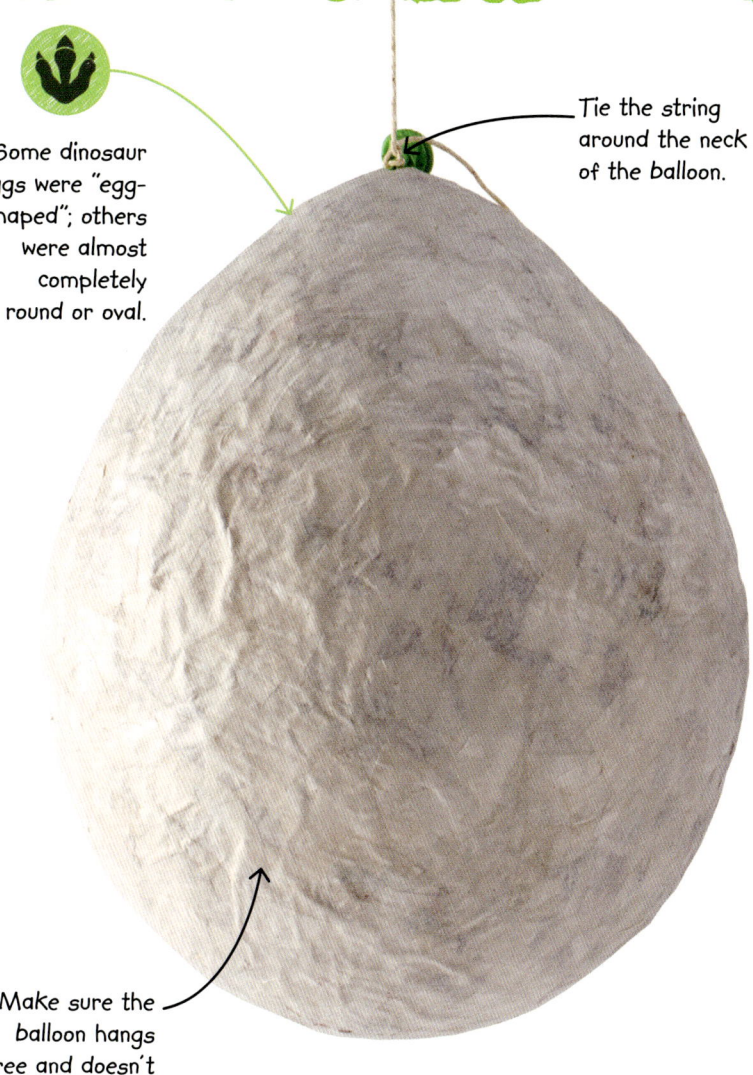

Some dinosaur eggs were "egg-shaped"; others were almost completely round or oval.

Tie the string around the neck of the balloon.

Make sure the balloon hangs free and doesn't touch anything.

7 Hang the balloon up overnight to let the papier mâché dry fully. Then repeat steps 3–7 so the balloon ends up covered with four layers of paper—printed, plain, printed, and plain.

6 Using the plain squares, repeat steps 3–4. As before, overlap the edges and take the layer right up to the neck of the balloon.

Using the plain paper helps you *see* which areas you have already done and which ones you haven't.

8 Once the papier mâché has dried completely, poke a darning needle or toothpick through the space near the neck to pop the balloon.

Take care not to damage the hole when you pull the balloon out.

9 After the balloon has popped and the air has seeped out, carefully pull the deflated balloon through the hole in the papier mâché.

10 To seal the hole, repeat the process of gluing layers of newsprint paper over that small section, starting with a layer of printed squares.

The papier mâché is quite robust, but brush gently.

Once you've finished, you shouldn't be able to see where the hole had been.

11 Alternate printed/plain newsprint paper as before in four layers, then leave overnight to dry.

12 Next, paint the egg with a coat of beige paint. Leave to dry.

Work in sections so your colors stay separate and speckled.

Dinosaur egg shells could be bumpy or smooth and may have had different colors and patterns.

13 Finally, dip a sponge into white paint and gently dab it onto a section of egg. Repeat with the beige and the dark brown paint to speckle the egg all over. Leave to dry.

GET CRACKING

You may find it easier to cut down to the line in strips from the top.

1 To make an egg that's "cracked open," follow steps 1–9 as outlined, but don't close up the hole at the neck of the balloon. Instead, draw a jagged line to mark where your egg will "crack."

2 Insert the tip of a pair of scissors into the hole and carefully cut down to the line you have marked. Cut away the top of the egg by cutting along the jagged line you've drawn.

3 Paint the inside of your egg with two coats of white paint, leaving it to dry between each coat. You'll need to repeat steps 1–3 if you want to make two "halves."

To cover up the newsprint, you'll need at least two coats of paint.

PREHISTORIC WORLD
IN THE NEST

Dinosaurs often laid large clutches of eggs, and there have been many fossilized nest sites found—some even have fossilized adult dinosaurs sitting on them. The biggest dinosaurs didn't sit on their eggs, incubating them in pits filled with earth and warm, rotting leaves instead. This egg was fossilized just as the baby dinosaur was about to hatch. In the same way that modern birds do, the baby dinosaur was "tucking", ready to push its way out of its shell.

Found in Ganzhou in China, this egg is thought to be between 71 and 66 million years old.

DIPLODOCUS AUTOMATON

With its amazingly long neck and even longer tail, *Diplodocus* is the perfect dinosaur for this clever machine. This project will awaken your inner engineer as you create the model's moving parts—which are all hidden inside that green box!

Diplodocus fossil bones suggest that it was an amazing 88 ft (27 m) long from nose to tail.

The head drops down as the tail moves up—to munch on some leaves or maybe take a drink?

Inside the box is a secret machine—one that you can build yourself.

The tail and head move elegantly up and down without you touching them—but how?

Turn the handle and *see* what happens ...

MAKE YOUR OWN
DIPLODOCUS AUTOMATON

For this project, you make a box, a model to sit on top of it, and a machine to go inside it. Your machine uses smooth cams, which are rotating shapes on a camshaft, to move pistons up and down. The automaton templates are half-size; the grid method on page 17 can help you scale them up.

Time 2½ hours, plus drying time

Difficulty Hard

WHAT YOU NEED

Pencil

Hole punch

Scissors

Smooth cardstock

Craft cardstock (⅛ in/2 mm thick)

Ruler

Masking tape

4 x lengths of dowel: 1 x 12 in (30 cm), 2 x 6 in (15 cm), 1 x 2 in (5 cm)

Paper fasteners

Paintbrushes

2 x 4 in (10 cm) pieces of string

Compass

2 x metal washers (with central holes wide enough for the dowel)

Acrylic paints in a variety of colors

White glue

Strong adhesive tape

AUTOMATON TEMPLATES

B
Attach tail in hole here

Body
Cut x 2

A
Attach head in hole here

Cam
Cut x 12

Each ¾ in (2 cm) square on this template is equal to 1½ cm (4 cm) on your grid.

A

Head
Cut x 1

B
Tail
Cut x 1

Neck

Handle A
Cut x 2

Handle B
Cut x 2

Piston end
Cut x 4

Right front leg
Cut x 1

Right back leg
Cut x 1

Left front leg
Cut x 1

Left back leg
Cut x 1

Stop
Cut x 6

Stop end
Cut x 1

Piston stop
Cut x 2

Tabs

Fold lines

BOX TEMPLATES

End panels on the main piece are the same size as side piece B.

Fold lines

| Side piece A Cut x 2 (10 in x 5½ in/ 25 cm x 14 cm) | Side piece B Cut x 2 (5½ in x 6¾ in/14 cm x 17 cm) | Center piece Cut x 1 (10 in x 6¾ in/ 25 cm x 17 cm) | Main piece Cut x 1 (21 in x 19 in/ 53 cm x 48 cm) |

Side panels on the main piece are the same size as side piece A.

1 Measure out the shapes of all the box pieces onto craft cardstock, as shown, and cut them all out.

Glue a second piece to each side to make it double thickness.

2 Score and fold the four fold lines on the main piece to make a box that's open on one side, and secure all the joints with masking tape.

3 Apply glue to one side of the box and stick on a matching side piece. Repeat for the other three sides and center piece. Leave to dry.

Where the two diagonal lines cross is the center point of the shape.

Make your marks in line with the holes on the sides of the box.

2 in (5 cm)

1⅜ in (3.5 cm)

4 At the center points on both of the two small sides of the box, push a pencil through to make a hole. Insert the 12 in (30 cm) dowel to check that it moves freely.

5 On the 12 in (30 cm) dowel, mark off 2 in (5 cm) from one end and 2¾ in (7 cm) from the other. Draw a rule across a long side of the box, in line with the holes, and mark off 1⅜ in (3.5 cm) from both ends.

6 Make a hole with a pencil at each of the two marks you made on the box in step 5. Check that a dowel can move freely through the holes.

A compass radius of 1½ in (4 cm) will give your circle a diameter of 3 in (8 cm).

7 Set your compass to a radius of 1½ in (4 cm) and draw the 12 cam circles. Punch holes where indicated on the template.

8 Brush glue onto six cam pieces and stack them together. Use the dowel to line up the holes, then remove it. Repeat for the other six cams.

The smooth surface will ensure the parts move freely, with no friction.

9 Cut two strips of smooth cardstock, 10 in x ⅝ in (26 cm x 1.5 cm). Glue a strip around the rim of each cam stack and trim the excess.

10 Position a cam on the dowel, over one of the marks you made in step 5, and glue it in place. Then glue the other cam over the other mark, attaching it the opposite way up.

Insert the long end through the left hole first, then the shorter end on the right.

This dowel will become a camshaft that turns the cams when you move the handle.

11 Next, insert the camshaft with the cams attached into the two holes on the sides of the box. Ensure it moves freely in the holes.

The squares are sandwiched by the body pieces and create space for the head and tail to move freely.

12 Copy all the remaining template pieces onto craft cardstock (using the grid method on page 17). Cut them out and punch holes where marked on the template.

13 Cut two squares of cardstock 1½ in x 1½ in (4 cm x 4 cm). Glue them together, then glue them *between* the two body pieces, lining up the body pieces and their holes.

To attach the neck, line up the holes marked A and push a paper fastener through them.

14 Slide the neck between the body pieces and secure it in place with a paper fastener. Repeat for the tail with the holes marked B.

15 Glue the front and back legs in position, as shown. Hold until the glue sets, then bend the leg tabs in toward the body.

The string won't slip through the tape because of the knot in it.

16 Tie a piece of string to one end of a 6 in (15 cm) dowel and glue it in place. Then make a knot in the string ¾ in (2 cm) away from the dowel.

17 Tape the string to the neck, between the knot and the dowel. Repeat steps 16–17 to attach the other 6 in (15 cm) dowel to the tail.

Trim the string pieces close to the knots.

18 Slide the dowels into the two holes on the top of the box and glue the foot tabs into position, as shown. Hold until the glue has set.

Glue a washer to the top of each piston stack to add extra weight.

19 Glue together three piston ends (with their holes in line) and a piston stop, then glue a washer over the hole. Repeat to make a second stack.

The dowels act as pistons, which move up and down as the cams rotate.

20 Put glue in the hole of a piston stack and push the head dowel into it, then repeat to attach the other piston stack to the tail dowel.

21 Glue three stops and a stop end together. Put glue in the central hole and push it onto the camshaft end outside the box below the head.

22 With the holes aligned as shown, glue the handle pieces in a stack. Glue the 2 in (5 cm) dowel into the hole on one side.

Glue the stops onto the camshaft below the tail and as close to the box as possible.

23 Stick the remaining stops together, then glue them onto the camshaft. Glue the end of the camshaft into the other side of the handle.

24 Paint the box green, criss-crossing your strokes and making the paint thicker and thinner in places for a dappled effect.

Add small patches of green, too, if you want.

25 Paint the *Diplodocus* a medium brown, then dapple on patches of paler brown and dot white spots all over the underside. Finally, add details such as eyes and shading around the head.

As the pistons move, they push the tail and head up and down.

The head moves down when the tail moves up *because* of the position of the cams on the camshaft.

Watch the pistons move up and down as the cams rotate.

26 Gently turn the handle to rotate the camshaft and make the head and tail of your *Diplodocus* move gracefully up and down.

PREHISTORIC WORLD
MOBILE NECKS

Plant-eating sauropods such as *Diplodocus* had astonishingly long necks, but the bones within them were full of air cavities that made them light. It used its long neck to sweep a wide area of ground so it could more efficiently eat without moving its large body. *Diplodocus* didn't need to chew leaves, but swallowed them whole, and they passed down that long neck straight into its stomach.

The long neck was supported by at least 15 vertebrae.

The whiplike tail may have been used for defense.

The head was small in relation to the body—with a comparably small brain inside.

TYRANNOSAURUS MASK

Want to be a *Tyrannosaurus*—one of the most powerful land predators that has ever lived on Earth? *Tyrannosaurus* may have roamed the Earth for about 2 million years, and its massive size, strong legs, and bone-crushing teeth made it a successful hunter. Make this fantastic mask and start practicing your roar!

Be a fearsome beast with this cardboard mask that goes over your whole head.

Make terrifying rows of sharp teeth to line your *Tyrannosaurus* mouth.

Use homemade stamps to create the skin patterns on your *Tyrannosaurus* head.

Tyrannosaurus jaws could crush bone. Fossils of their dung have been found full of bone fragments.

MAKE YOUR OWN
TYRANNOSAURUS MASK

You'll need a large piece of card for the main piece—craft cardstock or a large cardboard box is fine. Before you start, it's a good idea to look at the template and read the steps through so you understand how the different 2D shapes all join up to make the 3D mask.

WHAT YOU NEED

Pencil

Marker

Paintbrush

White cardstock

Craft cardstock

Kitchen sponge

Scissors

White glue

Acrylic paints

Masking tape

Ruler

Time 2 hours, plus drying time

Difficulty Hard

TEMPLATES

You can draw the curved parts freehand, but for the straight lines, follow the measurements below.

4 in (10 cm)

1⅜ in (3.5 cm)

Chin
Cut × 1

This edge forms the lower side of the mouth.

1⅜ in (3.5 cm)

Edge C

Lower jaw
Cut × 2

3 in (7.5 cm)

3¾ in (9.5 cm)

8⅛ in (20.5 cm)

155°

155°

Fold

135°

2½ in (6.5 cm)

130°

Upper jaw
Cut × 2

6⅛ in (15.5 cm)

140°

Point A

Glue area for attaching lower jaw

Fold

2 in (5 cm)

130°

95°

This edge forms the upper side of the mouth.

2 in (5 cm)

1⅜ in (3.5 cm)

Main piece
Cut × 1

4 in (10 cm)

3⅜ in (8.5 cm)

2 in (5 cm)

2½ in (6.5 cm)

8⅛ in (20.5 cm)

3 in (7.5 cm)

3¾ in (9.5 cm)

6⅛ in (15.5 cm)

Point B

Draw a row of jagged teeth for the whole upper jaw, then put to one side, ready for step 13.

Point A

Point A

4 in (10 cm)

1 Copy the template opposite to draw an upper jaw piece onto craft cardstock. Cut it out and draw around it for the second upper jaw. Cut that out, too.

2 Put the pieces upside-down, facing each other, on white cardstock. Draw a line between the point As, then draw jagged teeth along the whole jawline.

Try to get sharp, clean creases— you can use a ruler for this.

3 Fold the upper jaw pieces along the fold lines indicated. Put a ruler on a fold line, lift the card up against it, and press along the underside edge.

4 Carefully following the measurements on the template, copy and cut out the main piece. Mark all the fold lines shown.

Point A

Point B

Bend the card into a C-shape, not an S-shape.

5 Now carefully crease the main piece along all its fold lines. Make sure your bends are all in the same direction.

6 Line up the point A of one of the two upper jaw pieces with point B on the main piece. Tape them together.

Point A   Point B

Your flat, 2D pieces of cardstock have now started to turn into a 3D shape.

7 Carry on around, taping the two pieces together. Continue until all the straight edges of the upper jaw piece have *been* taped to the main piece.

8 Repeat steps 6–7 to attach the other upper jaw piece to the other side of the main piece; start by lining up point A and B as before.

Tyrannosaurus had a big, heavy skull about 5 ft (1.5 m) in length.

9 Turn the head over and run a strip of masking tape along all the joints to make sure everything is securely taped together.

10 Draw a lower jaw piece onto craft cardstock and cut it out. Then use it as a template for the second lower jaw piece and cut that out, too.

Edge C

Edge C

Tyrannosaurus had over 50 sharp teeth designed to puncture, tear, and slice flesh.

11 Draw and cut out the chin piece. Tape its short sides to the edges marked edge C on the template to make a combined lower jaw section.

12 Place the lower jaw section on a long strip of white cardstock and draw a row of jagged teeth along the entire length of the top edge.

If the teeth are a little *too* sharp, just snip off the tips to blunt them slightly!

13 Carefully cut out this strip of teeth and the strip you drew for the upper side of the mouth in step 2.

14 Apply glue to the outside of the upper jaw pieces, as indicated on the template. Stick the lower jaw pieces firmly in place. Leave to set.

Tyrannosaurus jaws had huge muscles to deliver a powerful crushing bite.

15 Add a strip of masking tape to the joint on the inside of the head, too, to make sure the lower jaw is securely attached to the upper jaw.

16 Next, paint your *Tyrannosaurus* head all over with a base coat of green paint. You may need two coats. Leave to dry.

17 Draw a couple of rough oval shapes—one larger than the other—on a kitchen sponge and cut them out.

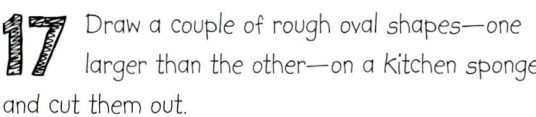

These ovals will form stamps to make patterns on the skin.

18 To paint the skin patterns, repeatedly dip the larger stamp in dark-green paint and dab it onto the mask.

You could even add a third color to give your *Tyrannosaurus* skin lots of texture.

19 Once those marks are dry, repeat step 18 but using a medium-green paint and the smaller sponge stamp. Leave to dry.

20 Paint an eye on either side of the head (make sure they're level!), and paint the nostrils on the front end of the upper jaw.

Tyrannosaurus had a really good sense of smell to help it sniff out prey.

21 Now paint the inside of the mask black. Start at the inside of the lower jaw and continue up into the whole head. Leave to dry.

A *Tyrannosaurus* bite was at least four times the strength of an alligator's.

22 Paint both strips of teeth black below the jagged bits so that they blend in with the black inside of the mask. Leave to dry.

23 Apply glue to the nonblack side of the lower-jaw strip, below the "teeth." Stick it along the inside of the lower jaw and hold until set.

24 Repeat this process to stick the other strip of teeth to the upper jaw so your *Tyrannosaurus* has two sets of fearsome teeth and is ready to hunt for prey!

This might be the last time you put your hand inside the mouth of a *Tyrannosaurus*!

Forward-facing eyes gave *Tyrannosaurus* 3D vision.

PREHISTORIC WORLD
ULTIMATE KILLING MACHINES

Tyrannosaurus teeth were bigger and stronger than those of any meat-eating dinosaur found so far. The biggest were 8 in (20 cm) long and more like tusks than teeth. They had sharp points capable of piercing thick skin and muscle, but were deep-set in the jaw and tough enough to bite through bone. Scientists think that *Tyrannosaurus* attacked by taking a crippling bite of its prey, which would then be seriously injured or die of shock, leaving *Tyrannosaurus* to rip it apart and devour it.

Thanks to its 3D vision, *Tyrannosaurus* was good at judging distances for an attack.

Serrations on the side of *Tyrannosaurus* teeth helped spread the force of its bite, giving it the power to crush bone.

TYRANNOSAURUS TAIL

Tyrannosaurus needed a strong, muscular tail to counterbalance its heavy head, so if you've made the mask, you'll need this impressive tail, too. Decorate it to match the head and complete your transformation!

You wear the tail like a backpack, with elastic straps over your shoulders.

If you've made the mask, just reuse the same sponge stamps to paint the skin.

Tyrannosaurus held its tail roughly horizontal so it could run on its powerful hind legs.

Use clever paper engineering to make this tail stand out by itself.

MAKE YOUR OWN
DINO TAIL

For a perfect fit, measure across your shoulders, and from shoulder to waist. Use those measurements for the back pieces, and double them for the width and length of the tail piece.

Time 90 minutes, plus drying time

Difficulty Medium

WHAT YOU NEED

Pencil

Paintbrush

Scissors

Craft cardstock

White glue

2 × elastic pieces

Masking tape

Stapler

Acrylic paints

Kitchen sponge

TEMPLATES

Tail
Cut × 1

End flap

Make the tail piece to size by doubling the measurements of your back and shoulders.

Measure across your shoulders, and from your shoulder to your waist, for this piece.

Fold lines

Spine—Cut × 2

Tab

Back B and Back C should together echo the shape and size of Back A.

Back B
Cut × 1

Back C
Cut × 1

Back A
Cut × 1

Cut these four slots.

The triangular cuts will make the upward curve of the tail.

1 Copy the template tail shape, cut it out, and bend the sides along the fold lines. Hold a ruler on the fold lines for extra-sharp creases.

You're making a series of three-sided shapes called triangular polyhedrons.

3 Bring two triangular polyhedrons together and tape them securely to each other. Repeat all along the tail, then tape up the end flap, too.

2 Bring two sides of a tail section together and secure the joint with masking tape. Continue along the tail, taping each section.

Make sure the pieces of elastic are long enough to fit over your arms and shoulders.

4 Draw and cut out the three back pieces. Loop elastic through two slots on Back A, as shown, and staple together. Repeat for the second loop.

Line up the fold of the end flap with the bottom edge of Back A.

5 Glue the tail end flap to Back A and tape the joints to secure the tail piece in place. Then pull the two elastic loops through the slots so that the stapled joints sit flush against Back A.

Back C

6 Draw the two spine pieces and cut them out. Bend their tabs in opposite directions and apply glue to each tab. Stick Back C onto one tab, as shown, and Back B onto the other.

A strong spine helped *Tyrannosaurus* hold its tail horizontal.

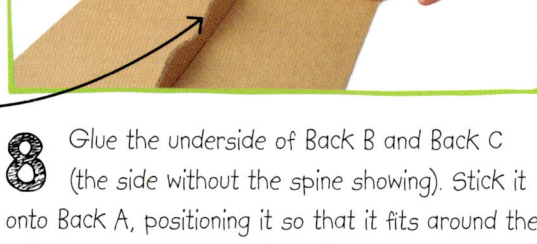

Line up the tail and spine so that Back B and Back C sit neatly over Back A.

7 Glue the two spine pieces together with the pointed ends of Back B and Back C facing the same way, so that they echo the shape of Back A.

8 Glue the underside of Back B and Back C (the side without the spine showing). Stick it onto Back A, positioning it so that it fits around the tail piece, and press firmly until set.

9 Paint the tail and back section all over with the same base color you used for the mask on page 93. Apply two coats if needed, then leave to dry.

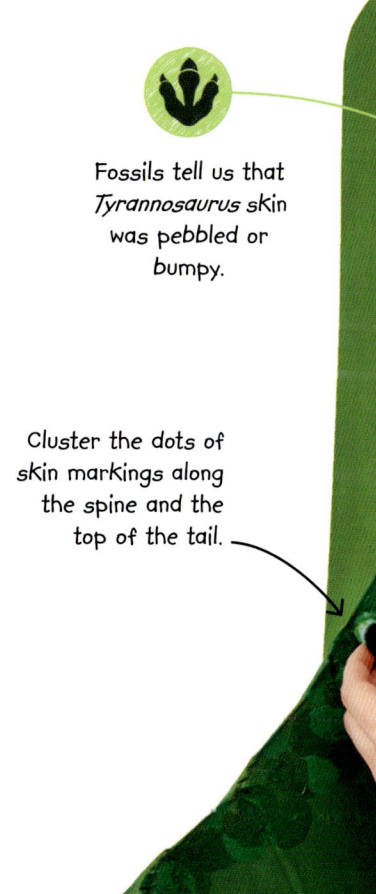

Fossils tell us that *Tyrannosaurus* skin was pebbled or bumpy.

Cluster the dots of skin markings along the spine and the top of the tail.

10 Follow step 17 on page 93 to make sponge stamps, or use the ones you made for the mask. Use the biggest stamp to paint dark-green shapes, then apply a medium green and any other colors you want with the smaller stamp. Leave to dry, then strap it on!

FOSSILS AND BONES

How do we know what we know about dinosaurs? Because of the fossils and other clues they left behind. Fossils are the remains of ancient life turned to stone, and they can reveal all sorts of important information about life on Earth millions of years ago. Create your own "fossils" as plaster, cookies, stencils, and jelly; make T-shirts and puzzle games; and enjoy exploring the exciting world of fossils.

PREHISTORIC BITES
FOSSIL COOKIES

Bake these edible "fossils" for a Triassic tea party. Fossils of dinosaur footprints, leaves, animals, and insects left important clues to what our planet was like millions of years ago. You could make these stamps for fossil footprint and ammonite cookies, then experiment with other fossil stamps, too.

Trace fossils were those made by animal activity, such as tracks, nests, or dung.

Use icing to color the footprints if you like.

Body fossils are those made by the bones or shell of an actual animal, such as this ammonite.

Dip your stamp in cocoa powder to add "mud" to your "fossil."

MAKE YOUR OWN
FOSSIL COOKIES

First, make the stamps; you'll need a polymer modeling clay that can be baked hard. Then get baking; this recipe makes 12 cookies. Ask an adult for help with the hot oven, and always wash your hands before making food.

Time 60 minutes, plus 10-12 minutes cooking time

Difficulty Medium

Warning Get an adult to help you use the oven.

WHAT YOU NEED

Baking sheets

White paper

2¾ in (7 cm) cookie cutter

Marker

Modeling tool

Polymer modeling clay

Scissors

Parchment paper

Egg

1 tsp vanilla extract

Large mixing bowl

Scales

superfine sugar 3½ oz (100 g)

Teaspoon measure

Wooden spoon

2 tbsp cocoa powder

Cup of water

Fork

3½ oz (100 g) butter

4 tbsp powdered sugar

Rolling pin

10 oz (275 g) all-purpose flour (and extra for rolling)

Green food coloring

Cooling rack

Tablespoon

MAKE THE STAMPS

1 First, make the footprint. On a piece of paper, draw around your cookie cutter as a size guide. Sketch a footprint inside the circle.

2 Roll small pieces of modeling clay to make the toes and pinch the ends into claws. Position them on your sketch. Make a clay heel for the foot.

Make sure all the pieces are stuck together well.

3 Use a modeling tool (or the back of a teaspoon) to blend the pieces together.

Use a modeling tool or the back of a teaspoon to blend the leg and the top of the foot together.

The underside of the foot should be nice and smooth.

4 Roll a small piece of clay and stick it to the top of the foot to make the leg.

5 Carefully turn over the foot to make sure the clay is fully worked together and the underside is as smooth as possible, too.

6 To make the ammonite fossil, roll a ball of clay into a long sausage shape with one end thinner than the other. Coil it into a spiral, and make sure it fits inside the cookie cutter.

7 Using the modeling tool or a fork, work your way around the spiral, marking straight lines across the clay.

9 Ask an adult to take the baked stamps out of the oven. Leave them to cool. The baking should have made them really hard.

An ammonite's shell enlarged as it grew, forming a beautiful hollow spiral.

8 Put the foot and ammonite onto a parchment-lined baking sheet. Bake in the oven, following the clay manufacturer's instructions.

MAKE THE COOKIES

Let the butter soften before you start so it's easier to mix with the sugar.

1 Mix the butter and sugar together in a large bowl. Beat the egg in a small bowl with a fork, then add it to the butter and sugar, a little at a time.

2 Once they are all mixed together, add the vanilla extract. Ask an adult to preheat the oven to 350°F (180°C/Gas 4).

Sprinkling a little flour on the counter stops your dough from sticking when you roll it out.

3 Add the flour a few tablespoons at a time and stir together until the mixture becomes a firm ball. (You might find it easier to do the last bit with your hands.)

4 Roll out the dough with the rolling pin until it's about ¼ in (0.5 cm) thick. Cut out the cookies with the cutter. Squish the leftover dough back into a ball, reroll, and cut out more cookies.

Remove the stamp carefully to leave a clear print in the dough.

5 Space the cookies out on parchment-lined baking sheets. Allow room for them to spread as they cook. Push a stamp firmly into each cookie.

6 If you want to make "muddy" fossils, dip your stamp into cocoa powder. Be gentle so that the cocoa powder doesn't go everywhere!

Move your cookies carefully so they don't break.

7 Once you have stamped all the cookies, bake them in the oven for 10–12 mins until golden brown. Ask an adult to take them out of the oven.

8 Leave the cookies for 10 mins before transferring them onto a rack to cool completely.

Add a drop of green food coloring if you want "swampy" footprints.

Make sure the icing goes right to the end of the toes.

9 Mix the powdered sugar with a few drops of water at a time until it forms a thick-ish pouring consistency. If you want a color other than white, add a tiny drop of food coloring.

10 Once the cookies are cold, carefully pour icing into the footprints you want to color. Allow the icing to set, then share the cookies with your friends and enjoy!

PREHISTORIC WORLD
HOW FOSSILS FORM

Fossils need certain conditions in order to form. First, the leaf, insect, or animal (such as this ammonite) need to lie undisturbed in mud or sand (sediment). As it decays, layers of mud and sand build up over it. Water seeps through the layers, replacing the decayed material with minerals that turn the fossil into rock. Millions of years pass. Eventually, glaciers or weather may erode the surrounding sedimentary rock to reveal the fossil.

PLASTER FOSSILS

A trace left in the mud—a discarded shell, a fallen leaf, a dead starfish or insect—over millions of years can turn into a solid rock fossil waiting to be discovered. Luckily, these fake fossils can be made in just a weekend.

Paint your "fossils" to make them look like they've been buried for millions of years.

Collect leaves and shells to make your "fossils."

MAKE YOUR OWN
FOSSIL

To create your fossil, you'll make a cardboard mold and use plaster of Paris—a powder that becomes a thick liquid when mixed with water, then sets hard like rock. For safety, ask an adult for help when mixing it.

Time
30 minutes, plus drying time

Difficulty
Easy

Warning
Ask an adult for help with plaster of Paris

WHAT YOU NEED

Pencil

Scissors

Masking tape

Modeling clay

Tablespoon

Cardstock

Cardboard

Shell or other "fossil" object

Acrylic paint

Empty yogurt cup (or other disposable container)

Plaster of Paris

Modeling tool or teaspoon

Cup of water

Kitchen towel

Paintbrush

1 To make the mold base, draw around your "fossil" object on the cardboard. Sketch a larger oval shape around the outline and cut it out.

2 Cut a strip of cardstock about 2 in (5 cm) wide and long enough to wrap around the edge of the base. Tape the strip all around the base.

3 Once you have attached cardstock all around the base, overlap the ends by about ⅖ in (1 cm), then trim off any remaining card. Seal the joint with a strip of tape.

Make the clay layer thicker than your "fossil" object.

Real fossils were created by imprints or objects left in mud millions of years ago.

4 Soften some clay in your hands. Press a layer of it inside the mold, deep enough for the object to be pushed into, then smooth it out.

5 Push your "fossil" object firmly into the clay to make a clear, clean imprint, then carefully remove it without damaging the imprint.

Let any leftover mixture harden, then throw it away in the container— do not pour it down the drain.

6 Mix up equal parts of water and plaster of Paris (about a cupful of each) in the yogurt cup (or any container you don't mind throwing away afterward).

7 Carefully spoon enough mix into the mold to make a layer of plaster about ⅖ in (1 cm) deep. Tap the mold on a table to get rid of air bubbles.

9 Gently remove the clay layer to reveal the "cast fossil."

8 Leave to dry for two hours, until the plaster is almost set, then carefully peel away the cardboard strip and the base of the mold.

The plaster has filled the imprint you made in the clay.

10 While the plaster is still a little bit damp, smooth the edges with a modeling tool or back of a teaspoon. Leave for 24 hours to harden fully.

11 Mix beige and white paint to make a pale rock color. Paint the fossil with a base coat, then leave to dry.

Cast fossils take their shape from spaces in mud filled by minerals that gradually turn into rock.

Wipe off most of the paint so it is only in the grooves and details.

12 Mix a little water and dark brown paint into a thin solution. Paint the fossil, then wipe much of it off again with paper towel. Leave to dry.

13 To finish, neaten up the final fossil by carefully painting around the edge with your original base color.

PREHISTORIC WORLD
TYPES OF FOSSILS

Although they all take millions of years to form, there are different types of fossils. Trace fossils are made by animal activity, such as droppings or footprints in mud. Body fossils form in impressions left in rock when a leaf or creature rots completely; if it fills with rock minerals, it's called a cast fossil. Sometimes, something is preserved whole as a true form fossil either in ice or amber (hardened tree sap).

Hard tissue such as bones can rot slowly to be replaced by rock-forming minerals.

Coprolites (fossilized dung) can contain clues about what dinosaurs ate.

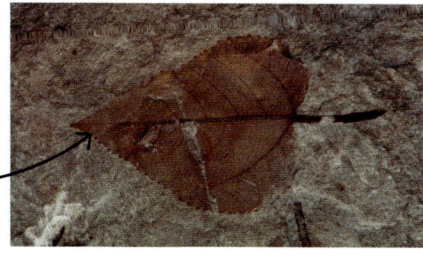

The impression of this dried leaf in mud millions of years ago even retained its color.

Choose whatever paint color you want for your fossil skull.

Using a stencil means you can repeat your pattern lots of times.

Try the scaling technique on page 17 to make your stencil in different sizes.

You can use two paint colors to give your fossil skull added "depth."

Tyrannosaurus fossils show that much of its skull was taken up with huge, terrifying jaws.

STENCIL POWER
TYRANNOSAURUS FOSSIL T-SHIRT

Body fossils of dinosaurs have helped fill in some of the gaps in our knowledge of how a dinosaur lived, moved, bred, and found food. Fill in the different kind of gaps between this stencil to make your own fossil-patterned T-shirt.

MAKE YOUR OWN
FOSSIL SKULL T-SHIRT

Stencils work by filling in the spaces between shapes; just remember to have connecting strips to hold the "holes" in place. Any cardstock will do, as long as its thick enough to stop paint from seeping through it.

Time
60 minutes, plus drying time

Difficulty
Medium

Warning
Ask an adult for help with the iron

WHAT YOU NEED

T-shirt

Stencil cardstock

Stiff cardstock

Pencil

Modeling clay

Masking tape

Scissors

Clothespins

Iron

Fabric paints

Stencil brush

TEMPLATE

Tyrannosaurus skull

The connecting strips are *very* important—they hold the stencil shapes in place.

Areas that are gray show where the paint will go on your T-shirt.

The gray areas are where you will cut holes in your stencil.

These are the connecting strips that hold the stencil together.

1 Draw (or trace) the skull template onto stencil cardstock. Make sure you include all the little connecting strips.

2 With protective modeling clay behind the cardstock, carefully make a hole with a pencil in each of the areas colored gray on the template.

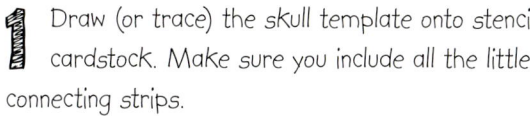

Take care around the connecting strips, as they create the holes for your paint.

3 Insert your scissors carefully into each of the pencil holes and cut out all the areas colored gray on the template.

4 Mark the width of your T-shirt on a piece of stiff cardstock and cut the cardstock so that it is as wide as your T-shirt.

The card is to stop paint from seeping through to the back of your T-shirt.

5 Pull the T-shirt down over the cardstock, sliding the card between the front and back to act as a barrier against the paint.

6 Smooth the T-shirt flat, then place clothespins down the sides to hold it securely in position against the cardstock.

7 Position your stencil where you would like it on your T-shirt. (We've done ours on the front, but you could put it on the back if you wish.)

Your stencil needs to be secured in place so the paint doesn't smudge.

8 Secure the stencil across the top with a strip of masking tape and press along it to make sure it's firmly stuck down.

9 Add another strip of masking tape along the bottom of the stencil to attach it securely in position on the T-shirt.

Tap the brush on the side of the dish to remove excess paint.

10 Dip your brush into the fabric paint and dab it carefully onto the T-shirt. Hold the stencil flat with your other hand.

11 Dab paint carefully all over the stencil until you have covered all the areas of T-shirt behind it. Leave to dry for around 15 minutes.

Move the brush up and down to tap paint on rather than brushing it.

Carefully peel off the masking tape once the paint is fully dry.

12 Mix a darker paint color and dab it around the edges of the stencil holes to give the skull some texture. Leave to dry.

13 Gently remove the masking tape and carefully lift off the stencil to reveal your fossil skull.

Tyrannosaurus actually had large holes in its skull, which helped make it lighter.

14 Ask an adult to iron the T-shirt for 5 minutes to "fix" the fabric paint so that it won't run in the wash.

15 Remove the cardstock and put your T-shirt on. You could reuse the stencil to make a whole herd of fossil T-shirts for your friends, too!

PREHISTORIC WORLD
WHAT A SKULL CAN TELL US

A *Tyrannosaurus* skull could weigh a hefty 1,100 lb (500 kg) despite large holes, called "fenestrae," that helped lighten the weight of it and made room for powerful jaw muscles. Large dinosaurs like *Tyrannosaurus* were at risk of overheating, and the fenestrae in the front of the skull housed huge air sinuses that probably played a role in temperature control.

A *Tyrannosaurus* skull was wider at the back to make room for the massive jaw muscles that powered its bite.

FOSSIL SKELETON PUZZLE

What does it feel like to discover a dinosaur fossil? Make this salt-dough skeleton, bury it in a tray of sand, then go fossil hunting for bones and try to solve the puzzle of what goes where.

Salt dough is modeling clay that you can make at home from just flour, water, and salt.

Work out how to assemble the individual "bones" of your puzzle into a complete skeleton.

Hide the "bones" jumbled up in a tray of sand, ready for a fossil hunt.

MAKE YOUR OWN
SALT-DOUGH DINO PUZZLE

Photograph or photocopy the template below and print it out at whatever size you want your dino bones to be. This project uses dough, but it's far too salty to eat!

Time
45 minutes, plus cooking time

Difficulty
Easy

Warning
Ask an adult to help you use the oven

WHAT YOU NEED

Baking sheet

Scales   Kitchen tray

1 cup of salt

1 cup of water

2 cups of flour

Large mixing bowl

Tablespoon

Modeling tools

Parchment paper

Oven mitts

Sand

TEMPLATE

Make a salt-dough piece for each of the black areas on the template.

The ball should feel like soft modeling clay when you have finished.

1 Mix the salt and flour together in a large bowl, then make a hollow in the center and pour in the cup of water. Mix it all together with the spoon.

2 Use your hands to knead the dough for about 3–4 minutes until it all comes together in a ball. Add a bit more flour if the mix seems too sticky.

3 Break off a small piece of dough and start molding the bones with your fingers or modeling tools—whatever works best for you!

4 Using your template as a guide, make and assemble all the different pieces of the skeleton puzzle. Lay the pieces in position as you do them to be sure you've made them all.

The bones are ready when, they're hard; ask an adult to check for you.

5 Lay the bones on a baking sheet lined with parchment paper. Bake them in the oven at 300°F (150°C/Gas 2) for about 30–60 mins, depending how thick the pieces are.

6 Once the pieces have cooled down completely, bury them in a kitchen tray filled with sand. Then begin the hunt for the bones of your fossil skeleton puzzle.

PREHISTORIC WORLD
A REAL-LIFE FOSSIL PUZZLE

Around 1909, in a quarry in Utah, paleontologists (scientists who study fossils) found a massive puzzle of fossil bones. About 150 million years ago, the site had been u river system, and the jumble of bones was probably the result of animals dying there during droughts. Now called the Dinosaur National Monument, it has a wall of more than 1,500 fossil bones from different dinosaurs.

FOSSIL TREATS
JELLY AMBER

A party treat made of hardened tree sap full of really, really old dead insects? That definitely doesn't sound like something you'd want to serve your friends, but they'll love this version, with jelly "amber" and raisin "insects."

This jelly mixture uses agar agar, a powder that absorbs water molecules.

Your "insects" are held in the middle of the jelly.

MAKE YOUR OWN
JELLY AMBER

This jelly uses agar agar, which is actually made from red and purple seaweed. (But don't worry, it doesn't taste like it!) It is vegetarian and comes as powder or flakes.

Time
30 minutes, plus setting time

Difficulty
Easy

Warning
Ask an adult to help you use the stove

WHAT YOU NEED

Silicone ice cube tray

Vegetable oil

Orange food coloring

Orange food flavoring

1 tablespoon agar agar powder

Pastry brush

Tablespoon

1½ cups (350 ml) cold water

Raisins

Saucepan

Toothpicks

Trivet

2⅔ cups (525 g) superfine sugar

Small bowls

1 Lightly brush the insides of the ice cube molds with vegetable oil. This will make your jelly amber easier to get out once it has set.

2 Gently squish some raisins to make insect shapes. Pull some into "spiders" or "flies," for example, and squash others into flat "beetles."

3 Add orange food coloring to the cold water one drop at a time until the water is amber-colored. Then add the flavoring a drop at a time, too. (You can taste it to check.)

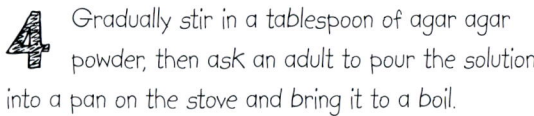

Stir until the powder has all dissolved into the water.

4 Gradually stir in a tablespoon of agar agar powder, then ask an adult to pour the solution into a pan on the stove and bring it to a boil.

5 Ask the adult to remove the pan from the heat and stand it on a trivet. Gradually stir in the superfine sugar, being careful of the hot liquid.

Real amber is made from tree sap that flows from a wound in the tree bark.

6 Keep stirring until all the sugar has dissolved and you have a completely clear liquid with no crystals in it.

7 Ask the adult to pour the liquid back into the measuring cup, as it is a lot easier to fill the ice cube tray from the cup than from the saucepan.

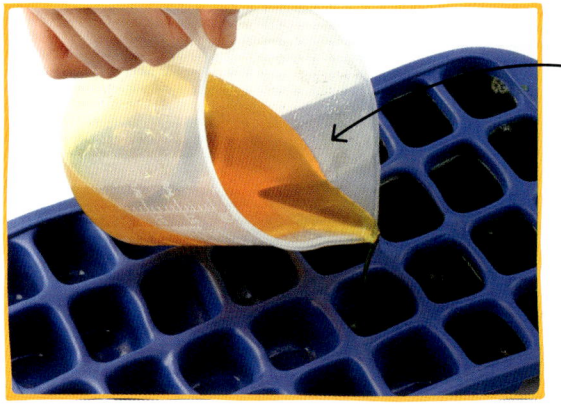

Pour carefully and steadily to smoothly fill the molds.

8 Carefully pour the mixture into each mold in the ice cube tray. Hold the measuring cup low to minimize the chances of creating air bubbles.

9 Wiggle a toothpick around in each mold if you need to dislodge any air bubbles. Leave for 30 minutes in a cool place to partially set.

If the jellies "bounce" slightly when pressed, they are ready.

10 After about 30 minutes, gently test with a clean finger to check that the jellies are partially set—no longer liquid but not solid yet.

11 Use a toothpick to gently push a raisin "insect" down into the middle of each mold. Don't push too far—just halfway down.

Amber fossils might contain insects, plants, animals, seeds, and even pollen.

12 After about two hours, when they have set completely, carefully remove the jellies from the ice cube tray to serve up your "fossil treats."

PREHISTORIC WORLD
THE SAP TRAP

Trees can produce a sticky liquid sap that hardens to become amber. Insects trapped in prehistoric tree sap before it hardened have been preserved so perfectly in it that even the veins in their wings are visible, like in the picture below. They look almost still alive, but they may be more than 100 million years old! And it's not just insects that have been fossilized in amber; scientists have found birds, a hatchling, and even portions of a dinosaur tail.

Carefully lift each jelly out by pushing the mold from underneath.

DINOSAUR PLANET

Wouldn't it be amazing to be a time-traveler and go back millions of years to see the Earth as it was when the dinosaurs roamed, grazed, and hunted? In this chapter, you can recreate that world for yourself. Grow a Jurassic jungle in a jar; build your own layers of "sediment," just like the Earth does; create an underwater hunting ground in a box; and make your own erupting volcano. It's thought that the reign of the dinosaurs ended when a giant meteorite struck Earth, so finish the chapter with your own meteorite experiment.

SEDIMENTARY ROCK CAKE

Sedimentary rock is the key to so much of what we know about dinosaurs and prehistoric life, as it is where most fossils have been found. Just as sediment builds up layer by layer, you too will build up your cake in layers. Then cut a slice and enjoy!

If this were real sedimentary rock, you might find a fossilized dinosaur in one of the layers.

Your edible "sedimentary layers" develop just like rocks, rubble, and mud do—but much faster.

MAKE YOUR OWN
SEDIMENTARY ROCK CAKE

Layer up cereals instead of sand and gravel, and marsh-mallows instead of mud, to build six tiers of "sediment" for this cake. It is very sweet, so serve it in small slices.

Time
60 minutes, plus setting time

Difficulty
Easy

Warning
Ask an adult to help you use the stove

WHAT YOU NEED

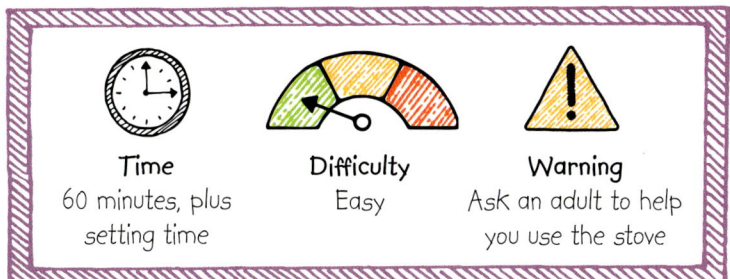

Pastry brush

Vegetable oil

Square dish

Saucepan

Scales

Trivet

Wooden spoon

3 cups (150 g) mini marshmallows

1 cup (40 g) cocoa crispy rice cereal

¾ cup (30 g) crispy rice cereal

1 cup (40 g) corn flakes

Palette knife or cake slice

3 tablespoons of butter

⅔ cup (100 g) white chocolate chunks

⅔ cup (100 g) dark chocolate chunks

⅔ cup (100 g) milk chocolate chunks

1 Brush the inside of the dish lightly with vegetable oil. This will stop the cake from sticking to the dish, so you can get it out easily.

2 Melt a tablespoon of butter and 1 cup (50 g) of mini marshmallows together in a saucepan over low heat. Take it off the heat as soon as they have melted and stir to blend them together.

3 Add 1 cup (40 g) of cocoa crispy rice cereal to the pan. They will become the first "sedimentary layer" of your cake.

Stir gently so your "rocks" don't turn to rubble.

4 Stir thoroughly to coat the cocoa cereal in the melted mixture.

5 Spoon the mixture into the dish and press it down gently to form a flat layer.

Butter and marshmallows are solids that turn into liquids when melted, but then set solid again when cooled.

Layers of sediment buried leaves and creatures that were then fossilized within them.

6 Sprinkle ⅔ cup (100 g) of white chocolate chunks on top and press firmly into the mixture. You have now made two layers of "sediment."

7 Repeat step 2, melting the same amounts of butter and marshmallows together. Then stir 1 cup (40 g) of corn flakes into the mixture.

Make sure the layer is flat and level into each corner.

8 Spoon the mixture on top of the white chocolate layer. Press firmly to crush the corn flakes and flatten out the mixture.

9 Sprinkle ⅔ cup (100 g) of dark chocolate chunks over the corn flake mixture and push them in firmly to make your fourth "sedimentary layer."

Stir gently again this time to avoid crushing your "rocks."

10 Repeat step 2, melting the same amounts of butter and marshmallows on the stove. This time, stir in ¾ cup (30 g) of crispy rice cereal.

11 Again, make sure the ingredients are completely mixed together, then spread the mixture on top of the dark chocolate layer.

13 Leave to set in a cool place for a couple of hours, then your sedimentary rock cake is ready to slice up and serve.

12 Finally, sprinkle ⅔ cup (100 g) of milk chocolate chunks over the rice cereal and push them down to make your sixth layer.

PREHISTORIC WORLD
THE LAW OF SUPERPOSITION

Sedimentary rock is where scientists discover the fossils that tell them so much about the prehistoric world. Traces of prehistoric life can be fossilized between layers of sand, mud, and gravel that have built up over millions of years. Geologists (scientists who study the Earth's structure and surface) know that these layers are created according to something called the Law of Superposition. That law states that each layer of sediment (or "stratum") is younger than the layers below it and older than the layers above it—just like the layers in your cake, with the bottom layers being the "oldest"!

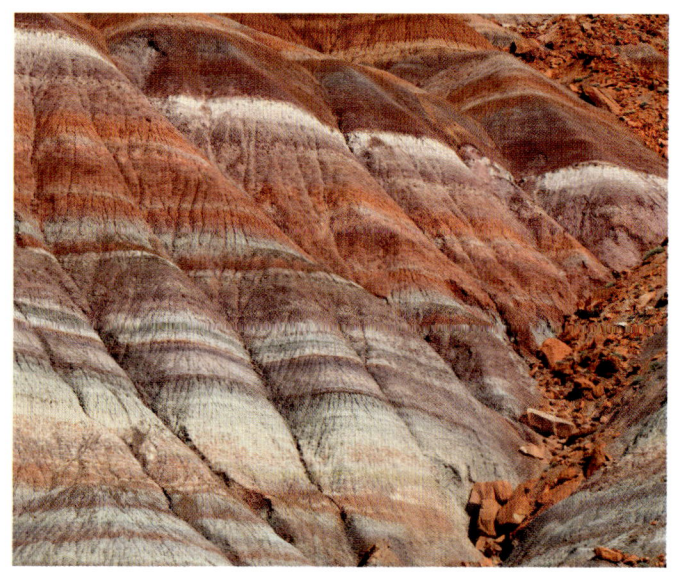

MARINE DIORAMA

While the first dinosaurs were walking on land, the Triassic seas teemed with marine life, including reptiles such as *Nothosaurus*, as well as sharks, bony fish, squid, ammonites, and many other creatures. How many can you fit into a shoebox diorama?

Almost-invisible threads hold the sea creatures in place.

Position creatures to fit their behavior; for example, this *Placodus* hunted for shellfish on the seabed.

Nothosaurus had to pop its head above water to breathe, so you could burst its head above the "waterline" of your diorama.

Making some ammonites larger than others creates the illusion that some are closer.

Three "layers" of seabed trick your eyes and create a sense of distance.

MAKE YOUR OWN
MARINE DIORAMA

For our diorama, we've used *Nothosaurus* and creatures that lived alongside it, but if you wish, you can research your own choices online. Think about scale and make some creatures smaller to trick your brain into thinking they are farther away.

Time 3 hours, plus drying time

Difficulty Hard

WHAT YOU NEED

White cardstock

Pencil

Scissors

A selection of acrylic paints

Thin thread

Paintbrushes

White glue

Ruler

Adhesive tape

Darning needle

Push pin

1 Paint the inside of a long side of the shoebox with sand-colored paint. This will be your base.

2 Paint the rest of the box with *blue* paint, inside and out. You may find that you need to repeat steps 1–2 if the box needs two coats of paint. Leave to dry.

3 Draw your main marine creature (we've chosen a *Nothosaurus*). Paint a base coat, then add dappled skin markings and other details, such as eyes and teeth.

Nothosaurus had webbed feet and stout claws, a bit like an otter's.

4 When the paint is dry, carefully cut around the outline of the *Nothosaurus*.

5 Repeat steps 3-4 to make all the other creatures for your diorama.

Draw larger plants on the narrowest strip and smaller plants on the widest strip.

6 Draw a rectangle the length of the box base and 2 in (5 cm) wide. Draw tabs ½ in (1.5 cm) wide on three sides, then draw two more strips the same length, but make each one a little narrower.

7 On each of the three strips, along the side with no tabs, sketch a wavy strip of *seabed* and plants. Paint the *seabed* a sandy brown, and use two shades of green for the plant leaves.

Making the plants smaller at the back creates an illusion of distance.

8 When the paint is dry, cut each strip out and bend the tabs away from the painted sides. Glue the three tabs of the widest strip to the sides and *base* of the box, near the back.

9 Next, glue the second strip into position about halfway inside the box. Finish by gluing the narrowest strip in line with the front edge of the box.

Make the two right-angled sides smaller than your *Nothosaurus* neck.

10 Hold the *Nothosaurus* in front of the box with its head "above water." Mark where the top of the box crosses its neck and cut there.

11 On white cardstock, draw a small right triangle. Add ⅝ in (1.5 cm) tabs on the right-angled sides. Cut it out and fold the tabs.

Glue the neck near one side, so there's room for the body inside the box.

This marks the spot where you'll stick the rest of the body.

12 Glue one tab to the back of the neck and the other halfway across the top of the box to hold the head "above water."

13 Measure the distance from the neck to the front of the box. Mark the same distance from the front on the underside.

Line the fold up with the cut edge of the neck.

14 Cut a strip of cardstock about 1½ in (4 cm) long and slightly thinner than the neck. Fold it in half, glue one half, and stick it to the body.

15 Glue the other half of the strip and stick it at the mark you made in step 13, lining up the neck above and below the top side of the box.

Make your holes parallel to the front of the box so creatures hang face-forward.

16 Tape one end of some thread to the back of your next creature. Thread the other end through a needle. Use the pin to make two holes, ⅝ in (1.5 cm) apart, in the top of the box.

17 Push the needle up through the left hole and down through the right one. Remove the needle and position the creature at the height you want it, with the thread hanging behind.

18 Tape the loose thread onto the back of the cardstock so that the creature faces forward when it hangs freely. Cut the thread to length, with the end hidden behind the creature.

19 Repeat steps 16–18 to position all your remaining sea creatures. Paint white splashes on the top of the box to show the *Nothosaurus* bursting out of the water.

PREHISTORIC WORLD ON LAND AND SEA

Nothosaurus was an early marine reptile of the Triassic period. Like a seal, it hunted at sea but probably came ashore to rest and breed. It could drive itself through the water with its powerful tail, but those webbed feet could also clamber over rocky shores. Its flexible neck and needle-sharp teeth were ideal for swinging through the water to snap up nearby fish.

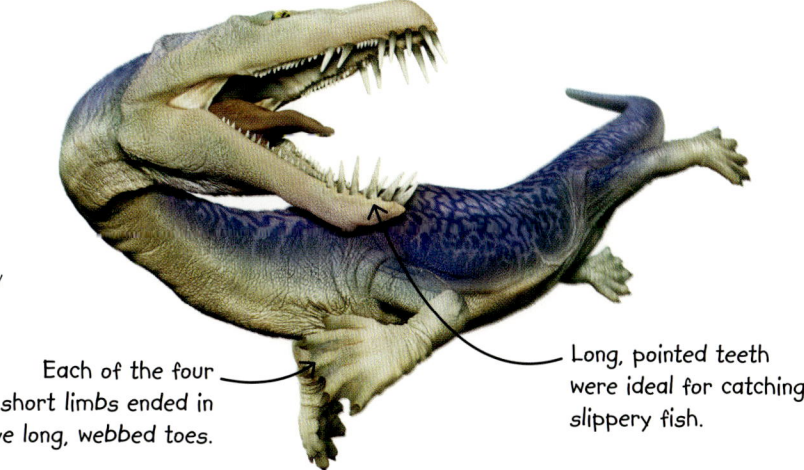

Each of the four short limbs ended in five long, webbed toes.

Long, pointed teeth were ideal for catching slippery fish.

JURASSIC JUNGLE JAR

There are plants growing today that would not have looked unfamiliar to the dinosaurs roaming Jurassic Earth. Learn about the plants we share with the Earth of 150 million years ago and create a mini prehistoric world in which your dinosaur collection would feel at home.

Have any small dinosaurs that need a home? They'll love this terrarium!

Collect small stones that will make great "rocks" for your mini Jurassic world.

Think about scale—
a small fern in a pot
can look like a tree in
your mini-world.

MAKE YOUR OWN
PREHISTORIC TERRARIUM

There are several small plants you can choose from that had Jurassic relatives, such as ferns, mosses, and horsetails. The amounts of grit and other materials below are approximate and will depend on the size of your jar and the plants you choose. Use a flat-bottomed jar if possible.

Time
30 minutes

Difficulty
Easy

These layers stop the roots rotting, so they can supply water and nutrients to the plants.

WHAT YOU NEED

Large glass jar (about 1 ft/30 cm high)

12 tablespoons of pebbles

13 tablespoons of sand

10 tablespoons of grit

Tablespoon

16 tablespoons of potting soil

6 tablespoons of small light-colored pebbles

Paintbrush

"Jurassic" plants   "Jurassic" toys   Small stones

1 Carefully spread a layer of pebbles about ¾ in (2 cm) deep over the base of your jar. Don't just drop them in, as they might break it.

2 Next, spoon over a layer of sand about ¾ in (2 cm) deep. Tap the side of the jar gently to settle it, then smooth it out to make sure it's even.

3 Add a ¾ in (2 cm) layer of grit, spooning it in carefully to avoid disturbing the sand. Again, smooth it out so the surface is even.

Scoop out a hole for each plant with the tablespoon or your hands.

4 Now add a layer of compost about 1½–2 in (4–5 cm) deep. There's no need to smooth it down, as you will be planting into it.

5 Carefully remove the plants from their pots and plant them into the soil. Think about how to arrange them so you can see them all.

Use a paintbrush to brush any soil off the glass.

6 Once you are happy with the positioning of the plants, add a final layer of light-colored pebbles around the plants. Take care not to put stones on top of the plants.

7 To finish, add a few slightly larger stones, your favorite dinosaur, or the fossils you made on pages 108–111. Water your terrarium occasionally—only when the compost looks dry.

PREHISTORIC WORLD
JURASSIC SURVIVORS

During the Jurassic Period, the Earth very gradually transformed from a hot, arid planet to become more green and lush, and some of the plants that grew then are very similar to those growing today. Ginkgo and monkey-puzzle trees, for example, have hardly changed since they first grew in Jurassic China. Modern-day ferns, conifers, cycads, mosses, and horsetails are all survivors of plant families that grew alongside dinosaurs.

CRYSTAL GEODES

Hidden in air bubbles trapped in molten lava as it turned to rock, or in air pockets between layers of sedimentary rock, there may be a secret—beautiful crystals called "geodes." Astonishingly, geodes have even been found in the spaces within dinosaur bone fossils! Real geodes take thousands of years to form, but you can make fake ones in a few days.

The longer you leave them to grow, the more crystals you will have in your geode.

Make your geodes in different colors, just like nature does.

MAKE YOUR OWN
GEODE

The key ingredient you need to "grow" your geode is alum, a chemical compound that forms crystals in water. The food coloring you add to the water gives the crystals their color. You can easily get alum at a pharmacy or online, but keep it away from your eyes and mouth and wash your hands afterward. Ask an adult for help with the boiling water.

Time 60 minutes, plus 12–24 hours soaking, and drying time

Difficulty Easy

Warning Keep alum away from eyes and mouth. Get help with hot water.

WHAT YOU NEED

Small bowls

Egg

Darning needle

⅔ cup (150 g) alum in a shallow bowl

Paintbrush

White glue

Egg dye

Tablespoon

2 cups (500 ml) boiling water

Protective gloves

Paper towel

1 First, wash your hands. Then, using a darning needle or toothpick, gently make a small hole in the shell of the egg.

2 Chip a hole in the shell just large enough to pour out the contents of the egg. Use the contents in cooking or throw them away. Gently rinse the shell in water and wash your hands.

3 Delicately remove more shell until just over half of it is left. Use your finger and thumb to gently rub or pull away as much as you can of the membrane on the inside of the shell.

Brush gently around the rim of the shell, too.

4 Cover the inside and the rim of the egg shell with white glue, brushing lightly on the delicate shell.

5 Carefully scoop the shell into the alum. (You may want to wear gloves for this.) Shake it gently to cover the glued areas with alum.

Shake off any alum that hasn't stuck to the glued areas.

6 Dip the rim in alum, too, then shake off any alum that doesn't stick and leave curved-side down on paper towel until the glue is dry.

Handle the packet of dye carefully.

7 Ask an adult to pour the just-boiled water into the alum powder. Stir to dissolve the powder completely in the hot water, then wash your hands to make sure there's no alum on them.

8 Empty your packet of dye into the alum mix. (If you want to be sure not to accidentally dye your hands, you could wear gloves for this step.)

9 Stir the mixture until the dye has completely dissolved, then leave it to cool down.

The longer you leave the shell submerged, the more crystals will form.

10 If you aren't already wearing gloves, put them on now. Slowly lower the shell into the solution. Be careful not to splash dye around.

11 Place the shell curved-side down, level, and completely submerged on the bottom of the bowl. Leave overnight or for at least 12 hours.

Take care— the crystals are fragile until they have dried.

12 With gloves on, carefully lift out the shell. The longer it is in the solution, the more crystals will form, so if you want more crystals, submerge the shell again for a few more hours.

Alum forms crystals as a chemical reaction with water.

13 Once you are happy with the amount of crystals on your geode, carefully put it onto paper towel overnight to dry fully. Throw away the gloves and alum solution and wash your hands. Then, why not make a whole collection of geodes in eye-catching colors?

PREHISTORIC WORLD
HOW GEODES ARE FORMED

Geodes form inside holes in rock. Over time (a very, very long time!), water containing dissolved minerals can seep through into spaces and eventually crystallize on the inside surface of them. Geodes often just look like rocks from the outside, but inside is a glorious secret world of crystals. Occasionally, a whole cave becomes a giant geode, such as the one in which this person is sitting—the Pulpi Geode in Spain.

What looks like a rock from the outside may actually hide crystals inside.

COLORFUL CRYSTALS

How a geode looks depends on the minerals in each rock cavity. Those minerals, carried by water that gradually enters the cavity, will determine what color and shape the crystals will be. Do what nature does and make your geodes in a whole range of beautiful colors!

Purple amethyst crystals may be formed when silicon and iron are present.

If the mineral celestine is present, crystals may be light blue.

If manganese is present, crystals may have pink tones.

Bright green crystals may be formed when copper is present.

Fine-grained quartz may form striped blue agate.

Agate comes not just in stripes, but in many colors, too, depending on the other minerals present.

LET IT FLOW!
ERUPTING VOLCANO

Dinosaurs didn't just have to worry about being eaten by other dinosaurs. Many also had deadly volcanoes to contend with—volcanoes that at any moment might erupt to release hot, molten (liquid) rock out of the top. Create your own "erupting" volcano, but stand well back when it blows.

A chemical reaction inside your volcano produces bubbling "lava."

Any dinosaur caught by the flowing lava had no chance of survival.

The cone of a real
volcano is made of
layers of solidified lava,
and it grows bigger with
every eruption.

This project is messy,
so work outdoors or
use a plastic sheet to
protect surfaces.

MAKE YOUR OWN
ERUPTING VOLCANO

Your "lava" is a foamy liquid produced by a chemical reaction using household ingredients: adding baking soda (a base) to vinegar (containing acid) releases carbon dioxide gas bubbles that become trapped in the dishwashing liquid.

Time
90 minutes, plus drying time

Difficulty
Medium

Warning
This project must be done outdoors

WHAT YOU NEED

Plastic sheet

Craft cardstock

Pencil

Tablespoon

Masking tape

Scissors

Sand

Large empty yogurt cup (or other disposable container)

White glue

White vinegar

Dishwashing liquid

Empty plastic bottle

Pitcher

Cup of water

Acrylic paints in a variety of colors

Red food coloring

Baking soda

Paintbrushes

Stick

1 Put the plastic bottle in the middle of a piece of cardstock and draw around it. Around the outline, sketch the shape of your "island" and cut it out.

2 Brush glue inside the outline of the bottle and stick the bottle in position. Use strips of masking tape to hold it in place.

3 Cut card strips that are taller than the bottle and wider at one end than the other. Tape them around the bottle, with the wider ends at the base.

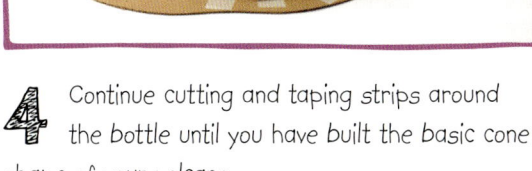

Secure the strips around the top with masking tape.

4 Continue cutting and taping strips around the bottle until you have built the basic cone shape of your volcano.

5 Add more strips to fill in the gaps, and trim off any bulky overlapping bits at the top to keep the shape of the cone.

Use an empty yogurt cup or other container you can throw away afterward with any left-over mixture inside.

6 Wrap a final strip of masking tape around the top, then cover the whole cone with strips of masking tape to ensure there are no gaps.

7 For the "rock" mixture, pour some sand into a large yogurt cup, add half as much glue as you have sand (a ratio of 2:1), and stir with a stick.

The opening at the top of a volcano is called the vent.

8 Add brown acrylic paint to the mixture and use the stick to work the paint completely into the mixture.

9 Paint the whole cone with the sandy mixture. Neaten the edge around the top, then leave it to dry thoroughly overnight.

Lava can *be* runny or thick— the thicker it is, the steeper the volcano.

10 Use a dark-gray color to paint a layer of "solidified lava" around the crater that trickles down the sides toward the *base*, too.

11 Once the gray paint is dry, dapple a green color around the *base* to represent the plants that would grow at the foot of the volcano.

The dishwashing liquid will trap the *gas* bubbles released by the chemical reaction and create foam.

12 After the green paint has dried, cover the rest of the *base* in sandy shades of yellow and leave it to dry.

13 Measure a tablespoon of dishwashing liquid into a pitcher with a tablespoon of *baking soda*. Stir them together.

Red food coloring will make your "lava" look like fiery molten rock.

14 Add 2 tablespoons of water to the pitcher and stir together. Pour the mixture into the bottle opening at the top of the volcano.

15 Measure a cup of white vinegar into a clean pitcher. Add a few drops of red food coloring and stir it thoroughly into the vinegar.

It's about to get messy, so stand well back as you pour.

The chemical reaction inside creates a bubbly foam that needs to escape—so it erupts out of the top!

16 Put your volcano outside and onto some plastic sheeting to protect the surface underneath. Carefully pour the vinegar mix into the top of the bottle.

17 Watch the volcano "erupt." The lava will pour out of the volcano. When the flow starts to slow, you could add more baking soda and vinegar to keep the eruption going.

Any vegetation at the base of the volcano will be smothered by the foamy liquid "lava."

PREHISTORIC WORLD
A WAVE OF LIQUID ROCK

Deep beneath a volcano lies a large pool of molten rock called a magma chamber. When underground pressure builds up, magma is pushed up through the cone of the volcano to erupt and spill out as lava, as shown here on Tungarahua in Ecuador. As it erupts, a volcano can send up huge amounts of ash and smoke into the atmosphere too. It was once thought that volcanoes might have killed the dinosaurs; however, scientists are now confident that a meteorite strike was the major event.

BRACE FOR IMPACT

METEORITE EXPERIMENT

Scientists think a meteorite that hit Earth 66 million years ago was probably responsible for wiping out the dinosaurs. Meteorites sometimes leave large impact craters when they hit the surface of the planet. In this experiment, you create your own craters to simulate the impact of a meteorite landing on Earth.

The way an object hits the flour and cocoa mimics the way dust and soil would fly up if a meteorite hit the Earth's surface.

Using a different-colored powder for the surface helps show the shape and scale of the impact zone clearly.

MAKE YOUR OWN
METEORITE IMPACT SITE

In this experiment, you create your own impact craters using balls of different sizes and weights, such as a rubber ball, ping pong ball, and marble. Find out which makes the biggest or deepest crater. Does the biggest object make the largest crater? Record the findings on your chart. Try dropping them from higher up too, to see what happens to the crater size.

1 Fill the dish with flour and smooth it out level so that you have an even layer that is about 2 in (5 cm) deep.

Time	Difficulty
30 minutes	Easy

WHAT YOU NEED

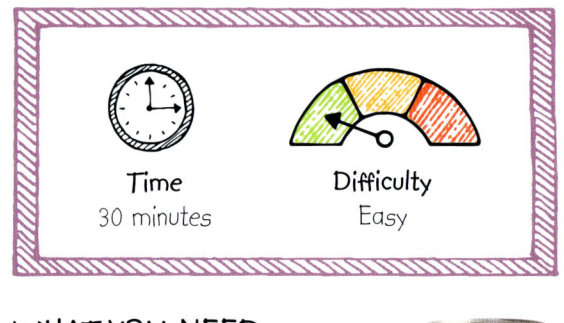
Large baking dish

Can

Long ruler or stick

Flour

Cocoa powder

Masking tape

Small sifter

Notebook

Balls or other sphere-shaped objects to drop

Ruler

2 Use the sifter to sprinkle a thick layer of cocoa powder over the flour. Using the two colors will help you clearly see the impact zones.

Object	Small marble	Ping pong ball	Rubber ball
Diameter of object			
Diameter of crater			
Depth of crater			
Shape of crater			

3 Prepare a chart for the results of your experiment. Make a column for each of the different "meteorites" you're going to drop.

Drop the objects from the same height so you're measuring them identically.

4 Tape the long ruler to a can and put it next to the dish. Start your experiment with the smallest "meteorite." Line it up with the top of the ruler, then drop into the dish and watch what happens on impact. Repeat with the other objects, keeping their "craters" separate.

Does your "meteorite" have a big impact on landing?

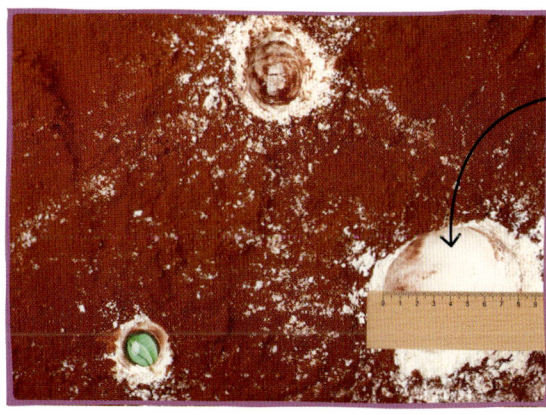

Measure the crater sizes, depth, and shapes with a ruler. What do you notice?

5 Carefully remove the "meteorites" without disturbing the craters they've made. Record the width, depth, and shape of the craters.

PREHISTORIC WORLD A DINOSAUR KILLER

These images show how the meteorite that hit Earth 66 million years ago may have looked as it whizzed through space, as well as the huge Chicxulub crater it made, 115 miles (185 km) across, as it landed. The 8-mile- (13-km-) wide meteorite would have triggered tidal waves and earthquakes and sent up huge clouds of gases, rock, and dust that blocked out the Sun and caused ecosystems to collapse. As Earth slowly cooled, it would have become uninhabitable for most dinosaurs—only birds survived, along with some animals, such as scorpions, turtles, crocodiles, and spiders.

GLOSSARY

2D
See *two-dimensional*.

3D
See *three-dimensional*.

AMMONITES
Marine mollusks with a coiled shell and octopuslike tentacles that lived in Mesozoic seas.

ANGLE
The amount of turn from one direction to another. You can also think of it as the difference in direction between two lines meeting at a point. Angles are measured in degrees.

ANKYLOSAURS
Four-legged, armored, plant-eating dinosaurs with bony studs and spikes on the neck, shoulders, and back.

ASTEROID
A space rock.

BASE
The bottom of a shape, if you imagine it sitting on a surface.

BODY FOSSIL
A fossil of the bones or shell of an actual animal.

CAM
A rotating shape that pushes or rubs against other parts of a machine to move them.

CAMSHAFT
A rod through a cam, around which the cam rotates.

CARNIVORE
An animal that eats meat.

CERATOPSIANS
Plant-eating dinosaurs, often with a bony frill at the back of the skull, such as *Triceratops*.

CONE
A 3D shape with a circular base and a single point at its top.

CONIFERS
A group of trees including pines, firs, redwoods, and cypresses.

CRETACEOUS
The era of time from 145–66 million years ago.

CYLINDER
A 3D shape that has a circle as its cross-section.

DEGREE
A measure of the size of a turn or angle. The symbol for a degree is °. A full turn is 360°.

DIAGONAL
A straight, sloping line that isn't vertical or horizontal.

EROSION
The breakdown of rock by natural forces such as water, wind, ice, or other rocks.

EXTINCTION
The dying-out of a plant or animal species.

FOSSIL
The remains of something that was once alive, preserved in rock. Teeth and bones are more likely to form fossils than softer body parts such as skin.

FOSSILIZATION
The process by which dead organisms turn into fossils.

FRICTION
A force caused by two objects that rub against each other.

GEOLOGIST
A scientist who studies rocks and minerals to find out the structure of the Earth's crust and how it formed.

GRAVITY
The force that gives everything weight and pulls things toward the ground.

HABITAT
The natural home environment of an animal or plant.

HADROSAURS
Large, four-legged plant eaters from the Cretaceous Period, many of which evolved flamboyant head crests to attract mates.

HATCHLING
A newly hatched baby animal.

HERBIVORE
An animal that eats plants.

ICHTHYOSAURS
A group of marine reptiles that first appeared in the Triassic Period. They evolved streamlined, dolphinlike bodies.

INCUBATE
To keep eggs warm so that they develop and hatch.

INTERSECT
To meet or cross over.

JURASSIC
The era of time from 201–145 million years ago.

KERATIN
A tough substance found in the feathers, hair, scales, claws, and horns of most animals.

LAVA
Molten rock that comes from a volcano; the same rock when cooled at the Earth's surface.

MAGMA
Liquid or molten rock beneath the Earth's surface.

MESOZOIC
The era of time from 252–66 million years ago.

METEORITE

An object from space, such as a rock, that lands on Earth.

OVIRAPTORIDS

Feathered, two-legged theropod dinosaurs with beaks.

PALEONTOLOGIST

A scientist who studies the fossil remains of plants and animals.

PARALLEL

Running side by side without getting closer or farther apart.

PERPENDICULAR

Something is perpendicular when it is at right angles to something else.

PISTON

A cylinder or disk that slides up and down as part of a machine.

PLESIOSAURS

Large, prehistoric marine reptiles that swam with flipper-shaped limbs. Some had very long necks and tiny heads.

PLIOSAURS

Short-necked plesiosaurs with large heads and powerful, toothed jaws.

POLYGON

Any 2D shape with three or more straight sides, such as a triangle.

POLYHEDRON

Any 3D shape whose faces are polygons.

PREDATOR

An animal that hunts and kills other animals for food.

PREY

An animal that is killed and eaten by another animal.

PROPORTION

The relative size of part of a thing compared to the whole.

PTEROSAURS

Flying reptiles that lived during the age of dinosaurs. The wings of pterosaurs consisted of sheets of skin stretched between the limbs.

RADIAL LINE

Lines that start from a central point are called radial lines.

RADIUS

Any straight line from the center of a circle to its edge.

RATIO

Ratio compares one number or amount with another. It's written as two numbers separated by a colon (:).

RIGHT ANGLE

An angle of 90° (a quarter turn), such as the angle between vertical and horizontal lines.

ROTATION

Turning around a central point or line.

SAUROPODS

Huge, long-necked, plant-eating dinosaurs that lived through most of the Mesozoic Era.

SCALE

The size of one thing compared to another; to copy something and make it bigger or smaller but keep all the measurements in proportion.

SEDIMENT

Small bits of weathered rock, minerals, and organic matter.

SEDIMENTARY ROCK

Rock that is formed by layers of sand and mud building up over a long time; the type of rock in which fossils are found.

SERRATED

A surface that is saw-toothed, like the edge of a bread knife.

THEROPODS

A large branch of the dinosaur family tree, made up mostly of predators. Theropods typically had sharp teeth and claws and ranged from hen-sized creatures to the colossal *Tyrannosaurus.*

THREE-DIMENSIONAL (3D)

Having length, width, and depth. All solid objects are three-dimensional—even thin paper.

TRACE FOSSIL

A fossil made by animal activity, such as tracks, nests, or dung.

TRAPEZOID

A four-sided two-dimensional shape with four straight sides, where two opposite sides are parallel but of unequal length and no corners are 90°.

TRIASSIC

The era of time from 252–201 million years ago.

TRILOBITES

A group of extinct marine animals without backbones.

TWO-DIMENSIONAL (2D)

Having length and width, or length and height, but no thickness.

VERTEBRAE

The bones of a skeleton that form the backbone.

WINGSPAN

The distance from the tip of one wing to the tip of the other when both wings are outstretched.

INDEX

ACKNOWLEDGMENTS

Smithsonian Enterprises:
Kealy Gordon, Product Development Manager
Jill Corcoran, Director, Licensed Publishing
Brigid Ferraro, Vice President, Business Development and Licensing
Carol LeBlanc, President
Reviewer for the Smithsonian:
Matthew Miller, Museum Specialist,
Department of Paleobiology,
National Museum of Natural History, Smithsonian

The publisher would like to thank the following:
Helen Peters for indexing; Dominic Elliott, Millie Hughes, Benjamin Torincsi, and Charlie Woodhouse for hand modeling; and Tanya Mehrotra for additional jacket design.

The publisher would like to thank the following for their kind permission to reproduce their photographs:

(Key: a-above; b-below/bottom; c-center; f-far; l-left; r-right; t-top)

31 Dorling Kindersley: James Kuether (clb) **41 Science Photo Library:** Mark P. Witton (br). **55 Alamy Stock Photo:** Jill Stephenson (br). **Dreamstime.com:** Mark Turner (tbr). **61 123RF.com:** Mark Turner (bl). **73 Science Photo Library:** Photostock-Israel (br). **79**

Dr Lida XING: (br). **95 123RF.com:** Leonello Calvetti (br). **107 Alamy Stock Photo:** B. Christopher (br). **111 Alamy Stock Photo:** Gina Rodgers (crb/Fish). **Dorling Kindersley:** Courtesy of Dorset Dinosaur Museum (crb). **Getty Images:** James L. Amos (br). **117 Alamy Stock Photo:** Antonello Lanzellotto / AGF Srl (br). **121 Alamy Stock Photo:** Chris Howes / Wild Places Photography (br). **125 Getty Images:** Layne Kennedy / Corbis Documentary (bl). **131 Alamy Stock Photo:** Ashley Lindsey (br). **141 Alamy Stock Photo:** Steffen Hauser / botanikfoto (br). **147 123RF.com:** fotointeractiva (ca). **Alamy Stock Photo:** Ingo Schulz / imageBROKER (cr). **Dorling Kindersley:** Natural History Museum, London (clb, bl, br). **Science Photo Library:** Javier Trueba / MSF (tr) **153 Dreamstime.com:** Pablo Hidalgo / Pxhidalgo (br). **156 Dreamstime.com:** StockSolutions (bl, crb) **157 Alamy Stock Photo:** Mark Garlick / Science Photo Library (cr), Science History Images (br)

All other images © Dorling Kindersley

For further information see: www.dkimages.com